Waking up in France

Waking up in France and surviving with a smile

SARA CROMPTON MEADE

Perspection Publishing, New Zealand

To my family

Contents

Prologue

My hands were sweating, my heart was racing. I could feel all these twisting, somersaulting bugs in my stomach, and they were really busy. I was in major panic mode because I was about to do something a bit uncomfortable. I was in front of 24 pairs of eyes, all watching me, all waiting for me to speak.

What if no words come out of my mouth? I asked myself.

What if I get completely muddled?

What if they laugh at my mistakes?

What if…?

I dithered, dallied and delayed.

I knew all of these people, but it didn't help. I laughed to myself for a moment, trying to distract my crazy nerves.

But now, it was now all up to me and I knew I had to begin. I couldn't delay it any longer. I took an enormous breath of air, gulped, swallowed and spluttered a bit, looked to Mum and Dad for support, and then began:

Bonjour ma classe de l'école St Exupéry. J'habite en France depuis septembre 2009, mais je suis né dans un autre pays. Aujourd'hui, je vais vous presenter, mon pays la Nouvelle-Zélande.'

And in English:

'Hello to my class at St Exupéry. I have lived in France since September 2009, but I was born in another country. Today, I am going to present to you all my country of New Zealand.'

Two years ago I arrived in France with my family. Two years ago I was the quiet, cautious kid, feeling alone and pretty afraid, and unable to say or understand a thing.

And now, here, two years later, I was speaking to my class. In fact, I was speaking in front of my *whole* class, all about my home country, and I was doing it in another language...*I was speaking French!*

Part I On leaving and arriving

Chapter 1 Me

Hi. My name is Matthew. I'm now 10½ years old. I've got grey eyes, lots of thick, dark, floppy, brown hair, and my parents say I look like I've got a cat on my head.

They say things like:

'Isn't it too hot to have that cat on your head?' or

'Shower day. Go and give that cat a wash!' or

'What's the matter, Matthew? Cat got your tongue?'

They think they are *so* funny.

When I'm older I think I will look a bit like the guy who plays Percy Jackson in the movies.

I live in a three-bedroom house in France, in a town called Ramonville St-Agne (pronounced *rah-mon-vil sahnt-ahn-yerh*) with my parents, my sister Olivia, and my brother Edward. I'm the eldest of us kids.

I don't really remember what I was like when I was little, but Mum and Dad like to tell this story about me. For some reason when I started learning to speak, it was with a *Scottish accent* and I could roll my *rrrr's* really well. It could have been because I had been watching SHREK – my all-time-favourite-green-hero-and-biggest-influence-at-the-time.

One night when I was about three years old I fell off my chair at dinner time.

'Matthew! Sweetheart! Are you okay?' asked Mum and Dad anxiously.

'Never*rrr* been better*rrr*!' I assured them, strongly and Scottishly.

Now that I am older (and my Scottish accent is mostly gone), my favourite things are building and playing with Lego and Kapla (wooden blocks), me and Edward riding bikes, scooters, rollerblades, and doing jumps at the BMX track, reading gazillions of books (mostly Horrible History books at the moment and I keep educating Dad on stuff he doesn't know), tickling Olivia, cooking and baking with Mum, watching music videos on YouTube, listening to Dad's CDs, and playing with my friends Thomas, Frédéric and Baptiste.

My *ultimate* favourite thing in the world though is watching Top Gear on TV.

I really like all the brilliant cars and the places they go, and of course Richard Hammond and James May are cool. I think Jeremy Clarkson is funny even though he is quite old. I know lots of stuff about cars now.

I suppose I'm just a pretty normal kid really. I can laugh my head off, have lots of fun, be a bit cheeky to Mum and Dad (but then I have to sit on the stairs), and sometimes I'm sad about stuff. Yep, pretty normal.

Oh, but I *definitely* don't like seeing blood – it's gross! And it makes my head all dizzy, and then my legs feel like they've disappeared and been replaced with wobbly jelly.

So what's so different about me?

Well, two years ago, when I was eight years old, we moved to France from our home country of New Zealand.

When Mum and Dad first started talking about it four years ago, I didn't really know what it meant. I was heaps younger then, and didn't know as much as I do now.

They used to talk about it when we were having dinner in our house in Karori, Wellington.

'Hey kids,' they would say, interrupting us from eating our apple crumble and ice cream.

'Dad is going to do some more study at university. How about we move to a new country to do it rather than staying in New Zealand? We can have an adventure!' (Dad was going to study for his PhD in Economics.)

They would say this in a reasonably-calm-totally-transparent-trying-to-be-cool-and-pretend-it-was-normal kind of way, even though they knew it would turn our cosy little life on its head.

'It will be such a *wonderful experience!*' they enthused. Olivia giggled and said, 'Oh, yes please!' while Edward just gurgled. He was only a baby.

Sometimes I started to cry because I think I realised it meant that I would be leaving all of my friends; I really liked my friends!

And I had just got my first badge at Cubs, and we had been on this exciting trip to see an emergency rescue helicopter. I bet they wouldn't have stuff like *that* in France!

'I don't want to leave New Zealand! It will be horrible anywhere else! I won't know anyone!' I would holler and wail. (I can be quite dramatic when I want to be.)

My parents would give me a hug and say stuff like, 'But darling, this will be such a *great adventure!*' and 'You will make new friends in France too, you know,' and, 'They even have Lego there, *and* we could go to EuroDisney sometime. How about *that* then?!'

Then they would tell me to finish my dessert.

You should also know this other thing about me. I can be a bit of a Rules Freak.

Whenever I go anywhere new I want to know all of these things, and more:

Number ONE: where we are going?

Number TWO: what time we are leaving the house?

Number THREE: what it is like there (is it in a big building, small building, inside, outside, in the city, in the country…)?

Number FOUR: who will be there, parents or just kids? and

Number FIVE: what *exactly* will we be doing, *in detail please!*

My sister, Olivia, is not like me at all – she LOVES new stuff.

She says, 'Yay! I'll get to make new friends and do new things! Hurry up! Let's go!'

I guess what I'm trying to say is that I didn't completely warm to the idea of moving countries. It's a crazy thing to do to a family I reckon; even crazier, when they don't even speak the same language in France.

They don't even speak English!

Did you know that?

What on earth were my parents thinking?!

Chapter 2 Moving house

It all got a bit more real when suddenly we were packing up our stuff in our house in Wellington and moving to a rented apartment.

Mum and Dad sold, stored or gave heaps of our stuff away. I had to watch Mum very carefully so that she didn't get rid of my precious collections of stones and shells from the beach, or sticks from the bush, or my drawings of robots. She can be a bit ruthless sometimes.

It was kind of exciting though, because I liked the apartment we were going to stay in until we moved to France. It was in a sort of community with lots of other apartments, and it had this great grassy playing area. The kids in the apartments used to hang out together, and ride bikes around the little roads.

My Mum really liked it there too, because it was quiet and she could hear the birds singing. She likes that kind of stuff. And she could keep an eye on us from the balcony and shout at us when we started getting up to no good.

One day though, a lady from another apartment gave me a note to give to Mum. Mum read it, and then went all angry-looking. She said something like, 'How utterly ridiculous!' and, 'What kind of place is this?' I really didn't know what was going on.

Apparently nobody was allowed to dry their washing on the balcony in case anyone else saw it. Ha! But my Mum *loves* stuff like drying the laundry in the heat of the sun and then carefully folding it later when it is still all toasty and warm. So sometimes Mum used to shout over the balcony – just a bit too loudly – things like, 'Kids, stop laughing!' or 'Kids, stop having fun! THERE MIGHT BE A RULE AGAINST THAT TOO!'

(To be honest, I think all that peace and quiet was going to her head a bit.)

I knew it was going to be time to leave New Zealand soon. Strange people kept coming to our house to take away more of our stuff, like our bikes, our chairs, our toys, and our furniture, leaving Mum with bundles of money and tears running down her face. She and Dad used to hug a lot and sometimes I would hear Mum quietly sobbing, 'There's so much to do! Why can't we just move to another city in New Zealand? Why do we have to move to the other side of the world?! Boo hoo!'

I wanted to comfort Mum but I didn't really know what to do or say. I wanted to hug myself too, because I felt like I was walking on ground that was shaking like a half-set custard; like nothing was reliable or steady anymore. I was '*okay*', but I felt really weird.

Dad was busy finishing his work. When he's not a student, he's an economist and has his own consulting company. Basically it means that he sits in his office at his computer, has lots of piles of paper everywhere and goes to meetings when he's not making gazillions of phone calls. Around this time he was also doing manly stuff like filling our suitcases with really big heavy textbooks, weighing them, muttering, tossing a few textbooks out, and then weighing the bags again.

And you know how dogs can get all jumpy and do strange things when there is an earthquake or a tornado or a tsunami coming? Well I think my little brother Edward must have sensed a change coming because suddenly all he really wanted was a puppy to keep him company. He was only four years old. He went on and on about this puppy. Mum would tell him, 'When we go to France we'll get a puppy.' (I think she said it just so that he would stop asking.)

One day Edward really, really begged, harder than ever.

'Mum, *pleeeeease* can we get in the car now and go to France and get a puppy?' Like France was a shop, or something! Mum felt really sorry for him and gave him a big hug and a hot chocolate. (He still didn't get a puppy though.)

The only weird thing that Olivia did was that she started speaking English *'wiz a veery 'eavy French akzent'*. I don't know where she got it from. Otherwise she was quite normal, which meant really excited about everything: you know, singing, dancing and drawing princesses with sparkly wands. Completely normal stuff for her, anyway.

One thing that annoyed me a bit was that we were only allowed to take one small suitcase of toys and our precious things away with us. We were selling lots of our toys so that we could use the money to buy more in France, and not have to ship them all over there. That was the plan, anyway.

Mine, an All Blacks rugby suitcase, *of course*, got pretty quickly filled up with Lego and marbles and books. (The All Blacks are New Zealand's national rugby team, *and* the current world champions, and we love them!)

Olivia filled her suitcase with Barbie dolls, her wool for knitting and her arty stuff, and Edward took his dinosaurs and zillions of stuffed toys. He's a stuffed-toy-kind-of-guy.

As I said, we weren't going to ship any massive containers of our stuff to France or anything like that. Oh no! Instead, we were going to take SIXTEEN SUITCASES!

Dad had found out that if you fly through the USA or Canada you could take double your normal weight allowance for your suitcases plus he had a couple of extra bags that he could take with his airpoints-membership-system-thing.

So our big house was reduced to only 16 suitcases (which is quite a lot when you are trying to stuff them all into the back of one car. *To be precise*, as Thomson and Thompson would say; they don't fit.)

Chapter 3 Goodbye Wellington

One weekend Mum and Dad had this big farewell party at the Anglican Church hall in Wadestown, Wellington. There was lots of yummy French food that our friend Stéphane had prepared. He's a real French chef in Wellington! The party went on for hours.

It didn't really feel like a goodbye-everyone-party to me, actually more like an eat-heaps-drink-lots-run-around-madly-with-all-my-friends-party.

Dad made up these massive posters of where we were going in France though, and he had maps and pictures on the wall for people to look at. I thought that was quite a good idea because I could show my friends – again – how far we were going to be flying. Lots of people showed us where they had been to in France too.

We had just enough time before we left New Zealand to go and see a rugby match in Wellington between the All Blacks and France at the Westpac Stadium. It was pretty amazing, probably because I had never seen so many people in one place before.

Crikey! It was really noisy, and really cold, but New Zealand won and we were happy!

And to make it more interesting and memorable, someone had smuggled in a chicken painted in the French colours (blue, white and red – *bleu, blanc et rouge*) and it was running around the field. I have to tell you that a wet and worried chicken is very difficult to catch. Olivia felt a bit sorry for that chicken.

I remember our last day at school really well. We were going to a Montessori school where they have combined ages in the same classroom.

That meant my sister and I were in the same class, called Pohutukawa (that's the name of a tree in New Zealand that has dark green leaves and red flowers. The flowers bloom at Christmas time so it is called 'the New Zealand Christmas tree', and we even sang a song about it at my Montessori preschool.)

'Now class, please listen to me,' said my teacher. 'As you know, Matthew and Olivia are moving to another country. Does anyone know where they are going? Hands up if you know.'

'No, Johnny. They are not moving to Canada. *You* and *your* family are moving to Canada at the end of the year. Does anyone else know? Ryan?'

'Yes, that's right, well done Ryan. They are moving to France. Mathis, Charles, do you know what language they speak in France?'

'*Oui, maîtresse, ils parlent français en France,*' said Mathis and Charles together; in perfect French!

They had said, 'Yes, they speak French in France.' Mathis and Charles could both speak French because Mathis was born in France, and Charles' Swiss Mum could speak French. Incredible, I thought!

Then I showed the class on the globe where France was. Yep, there it was, on the other side of the world – actually *completely* on the other side. Each time I saw it, it kind of made me bubble up with tears inside. But I giggled and jumped around a bit and the tears would go away.

Then the class gave me and Olivia a little booklet each that all the kids had written messages in, with a photo of everyone, which was cool. The Principal, Mr Wilson, even came and said goodbye to us, and gave us a certificate and a hug. He was really nice.

Here's what some of the kids wrote in my booklet (I haven't changed any of the funny spelling!):

'Thank you Matthew for playing whith me. I would also like to thank you for being one off the most helpfull ones in the class. From Claire.'

'I like it how you play nisely, and I will miss you Matthew from Paul'.

'To Matthew I hope you have a grate time in france and I really injoid playing with you from Charles.'

'I don't no what to say, Gerard.'

Edward had said goodbye to the kids and teachers in his Montessori preschool, and had given them a book to remember him by (*Herbert the Brave Sea Dog*). He did the Roman arch one last time because he really loved doing that.

And then we said goodbye. Olivia was giving her friends lots of hugs, Mum looked like she was going to cry and Dad was really brave – like normal.

So, that was the end of my life in the Montessori classroom at Otari Primary School, Wellington. I knew I would be able to visit everyone again, but man, it felt really bizarre.

The night before we left New Zealand, things got a bit too exciting though.

'Mum, Dad, come quick! Edward's coughing and choking!' shouted Olivia from the bathroom. We all raced in to see what was happening.

Apparently Edward had decided to take a slurp of Dad's aftershave and had to go to the After Hours Medical Centre that very night to make sure he was okay. He was: it was only a *tiny* amount of aftershave. Phew! We were all a bit worried.

Afterwards Edward said to Dad, 'I will never, ever, ever do that again, 'cos it didn't taste nice at all.' He was very serious too. He had got a big fright too.

Our last day in Wellington was a sunny day. We walked around Oriental Bay next to the sea and had a nice lunch at our favourite café by Waitangi Park so that we could go to Te Papa, the Museum of New Zealand, *one last time*. (It's great there, and if you haven't been there, you should! There's so much stuff for kids to do and see.)

We managed to get all our suitcases to the airport, only because a kind man in a taxi van helped us. Dad had to give him lots of money in return though. But all those towering suitcases meant that the airport trolleys were piled so high I seriously thought they were going to fall over.

Some nice friends, plus Nana and Uncle Chris, came to say goodbye to us. There were lots of hugs and kisses and goodbyes from us all.

'Bye bye Nana! We'll miss you!'

'We love you!'

'Farewell everyone!'

'Good luck!'

'Bon voyage!'

Chapter 4 The flights

We made it to Auckland. That was the easy part. From there we were going to catch our plane to Vancouver, Canada and then fly to Germany, and finally to Toulouse, France (pronounced *too-loose*).

Granna and Grandpa were waiting to say goodbye to us at the airport in Auckland and it was really great to see them. They gave us some tic tacs (sweets that we really liked). I remember that because that was the first time I had had a box of tic tacs *all for myself*.

'Goodbye chickies!' cooed Granna lovingly, as she crushed us in her embrace. 'Enjoy every minute, won't you?!'

'Goodbye you great kids. See you in a year,' said Grandpa. I felt massively bad and sad about leaving them though because they are so ancient and, to be honest with you, they could stop breathing at any moment. That worried me a bit.

We hugged and hugged them for ages until it was time to go. Mum was crying *again*. I think she thought it might be the last time she would see them, and she was also freaking out because she doesn't like being in 'enclosed spaces' (like planes) for very long. She calls it 'claustrophobia'.

And then we sat in the plane waiting to leave for ages and ages. 'Dad, is it normal to wait this long?' I asked.

Finally an announcement was made.

Some nice man said, 'Ladies and gentlemen, boys and girls. This is your Senior Cabin Steward speaking. We're very sorry for the delay folks but we've had one of the water heaters explode in the galley and there's water dripping all through the electrical wiring. Not the sort of thing that you want to happen on an aeroplane! (Ha ha ha!) But don't worry, the engineer's onto it. He'll just get that sorted and then we'll be on our way…'

I did *not* like the sound of that one bit!

'Dad, Dad, are we all going to die?' I wanted to shout.

Mum was always saying to me 'Don't panic, Mr Mannering!' and I didn't understand what she meant, but I sure did want to panic right then! I think she did too. Her eyes got really big and she just stared at Dad without saying anything. Dad just shrugged, like, 'Yeah, whatever.'

But inside, Dad was thinking that 'explosion' and 'plane' and 'water' and 'electricity' in the same sentence was not really a great way to start a long flight across the Pacific Ocean for 11 hours, if you know what I mean. He just figured that the pilot must want to stay alive too, so we wouldn't be flying unless it was safe.

Us kids got served our meals first (but you have to book it in advance) which was a *privilege* Dad said. We finally got to eat at 10.30 pm. That didn't feel much like a privilege to me because I was STARVING! We were also given these packs of fun-things-to-do-on-a-plane which kept us amused for a good five or six minutes.

But, actually, the best thing about the flights were these great TVs in the back of the next person's seat, so you could plug in your headphones and choose what you wanted to watch or listen to without your Mum or Dad yelling at you to turn-it-down-why-don't-you?!

Many, many blurry hours later we arrived in Vancouver, Canada. It was weird looking down from the plane onto this city I had never seen before.

Dad said he didn't want us to fly through the USA so that we wouldn't have the hassle of being searched at customs as if we were terrorists, and definitely not with all of our suitcases. I had never been on a really long flight like that to a whole new country. I had only ever been to Australia, and that is really close by; only about three hours away.

Edward was looking all dopey and droopy, and his eyes were half shut. As the announcement was made that we had to put our seats up straight, Edward murmured to Dad, 'Have we left Wellington yet?' I don't think he knew *who* he was or *where* he was.

We hung around in Vancouver for a while (*quite a while*), and then we flew to Munich which is in Germany. On this plane they had these downstairs toilets, which I thought was completely cool.

There suddenly seemed to be a lot of people speaking different languages (they all sounded different anyway). Mum said she could hear French, German and English. Cool! I noticed that the flight attendants could choose which language to use when they spoke to a passenger just by looking at them! They must have been psychic or had super-memory powers from aliens or something, a bit like Mum I guess. She's always kind of knows who's knocking at the door before she sees them, or calling on the telephone. She can tell by the way the phone rings, or so she says. *And* she has eyes in the back of her head…

I was really, really tired by now because I had watched as many movies as I could on the last flight. We weren't able to all sit together on this flight so I was sitting by myself in front of Dad. I fell asleep on the man's arm next to me. He said it was okay when Mum asked him, and he was really nice because he kept checking on me to make sure my blanket was still on me and that I wasn't snorting or dribbling too much.

We arrived in Germany, and after another wait we finally arrived in Toulouse which is in the south-west of France. FACT TIME: 36 hours after we had left Wellington, New Zealand, we arrived in France. We had been flying in airplanes for 25 hours, plus *lots of waiting* at the airports.

Poor Edward didn't know where he was again. 'Are we in France yet Dad?' he asked, sleepily, as we hauled our exhausted bodies into the taxi van.

'Can't you see that all the signs are in another language, Edward?!' I asked him, just a little bit impatiently. He didn't say anything: I think he was too stunned.

'Oh, that's right, sorry Edward,' I said. 'You can't read yet,' I whispered quietly, feeling a bit bad.

Dad had booked a big taxi van to meet us to take us and our luggage to where we were staying. We were really lucky because *most* of our suitcases arrived, and we only had to stay at the airport for one more hour sorting out the paperwork to try and find the two missing suitcases (including Dad's precious electric guitar). The taxi driver helped us fill out the form in French.

Edward was crying and crying now and Olivia was like really hyper. I felt like I had crashed my BMX bike into a big wall of tyres really fast.

Chapter 5 Bonjour la France!

Do you know what a château is? It's a castle! We were staying in a 16th century castle!

Well, it was more like a grand house than a castle, but that's what this one was called, the Château de la Cépière (pronounced *sha-toe der lah se-pee-yeah*).

A friend of Dad's from New Zealand, James, was studying in the same PhD programme as Dad, only a few years ahead. He had a room in an apartment in this château and he said that we could stay there when we arrived. Nice guy!

Our first day in France was pretty mind-boggling. It was like this buzzy-vibration of newness which would normally freak me out, but because I was in this spaced-out zone it seemed to be okay. And Mum and Dad were with me of course. James and his girlfriend took us to a big market outside this enormous old church called Saint Aubin (pronounced *sahnt orh-bah*), in the middle of Toulouse city.

Talk about another world! It was really, really crowded and it all smelt different. There were lots and lots of little market stalls everywhere selling fresh fruits and vegetables, different breads, meat, clothes – everything!

Olivia noticed that there were lots of doggie-do-dos everywhere on the ground, so we had to be quite careful where we put our feet. In New Zealand we would have sat on the grass for lunch, but we couldn't because of all the doggie-do-dos and the beer cans, so we ate pizza on the cathedral steps instead.

We watched all the people going by and listened to the hum and murmur of different languages. There were lots of dark-skinned people too, from Algeria, Morocco, Tunisia, and from other countries in Africa, Dad told me. You don't see many people who look like that in New Zealand (usually European, Māori, Pacific Island or Chinese people there).

Then suddenly, 'Dad, help! We're going to crash!' I yelped at Dad, certain that death was approaching us faster than a speeding train. Actually it *was* a speeding train that was approaching us, but we weren't going to die.

We were on the underground metro that goes through these long tunnels under Toulouse. But the weird thing is, the trains DON'T EVEN HAVE A DRIVER! It's really spooky because it looks like they drive all by themselves. And fast! It's awesome when two trains pass each other in the tunnel, at high speed, with no drivers. It looks so crazy.

Dad says it's all automated and that there are some highly-qualified people sitting in a room somewhere checking that the computer system is sending the trains to the right station at the right time.

Phew, that's a relief, I thought. But then I wondered what would happen if all of the highly-qualified people needed to pee at once, or they all went out for their Christmas lunch together, or something like that. What would happen to the trains??

I'm *so good* at worrying about all sorts of things.

It was really hot in Toulouse – over 30 degrees Celsius (over 86 degrees Fahrenheit) – and we arrived at the start of autumn when it was supposed to be a bit cooler. Ha!

(It was the start of spring in New Zealand. Everything here really was upside-down; even the seasons!)

It was really weird having this thing called 'jetlag' too. It's when your body kind of doesn't know what time it is. Mum thinks it's when your soul takes a little while to catch up with your body after travelling really fast over a long distance. Weird! But we all felt rather strange.

We were always saying things like, 'Is it time for breakfast?'

'Is it okay to be running around outside, Dad?'

'Should I be sleeping when it's dark even though I don't feel tired?'

'Mum, why can't I stay awake after five in the after…zzzzzzz…'

It took a few days and nights to adjust.

The château had an enormous garden and enormous trees. It was really nice. There were lots of places that we could play, although it was hard being quiet all the time because the ground floor of the château was used by real live businesses with real live French people trying to work.

It didn't help that Edward kept falling over, or falling out of a tree, or screaming his head off if Olivia didn't want to play with him. Mum got quite flustered when the real live, very concerned, business people kept rushing out to see if Edward was okay.

'Zees boy, 'e keeps cry-ing. 'e eez ok?'

One day, when we were all still really jetlagged, Mum and us kids went into Toulouse city. We saw this stone bridge called Pont Neuf which means the 'new bridge'. I thought that was really funny because it was built in the 16th century which is not exactly new! I guess it was newer than the ones before it though as they had been made of wood and kept being washed away in floods.

Anyway, we had just walked over Pont Neuf and Mum said she saw some familiar-looking people.

She had a sudden urge to say *Kia ora* to them. That's the phrase for 'hello' for the Māori people of New Zealand. Suddenly, these four big Māori or possibly Pacific Island guys spun around in surprise and said *Kia ora* back to Mum!

Well, normally Mum is quite friendly and will stop and talk to people, and so later I asked her, 'Why did you keep on walking Mum? Why didn't you stop and talk to those guys? I think they were from New Zealand!'

What she told us was really funny. She said that she thought she wouldn't be able to speak to them *because her French wasn't good enough*!

Huh?! I thought. The aliens have really got her this time.

It was when she was quite a way down the street that she realised that *they would have spoken English*. Oh man! She had only been in France for a few days but her head was telling her that she couldn't speak the same language as all the people she was looking at – odd, huh? (Grandpa would say that her brain was definitely completely 'muxed-ip'). Later we saw some advertising for a rugby sevens match against New Zealand, and we reckon those big guys might have been part of the team.

The nearest supermarket to the château sold food that was quite different to what we were used to. They had a great bakery and we used to walk there each day to buy something sweet and yummy for morning tea, like a *pain-au-chocolat* (soft buttery bread with chocolate inside, called a *chocolatine* in the Toulouse area). Yum!

We noticed that lots of food was packaged up in plastic containers and wrapped in plastic wrap, way more than in New Zealand.

A couple of times we bought broccoli that was wrapped in plastic and maybe two minutes after we took the wrap off, the broccoli started turning yellow. I don't think it was very fresh and we didn't buy it after that.

We could buy kiwifruit that had come all the way from New Zealand though, which was great. The French people just call them 'kiwi', not 'kiwifruit' like we do.

The supermarket also had a special system if you wanted to buy meat from the butcher. You would take a ticket and wait for your number to be called out. Mum wasn't brave enough to do that. The butcher sold these skinned rabbits that still had their eyes in, and they were open! Completely freaky! He also sold these monster ginormous chickens that we found out later were turkeys.

The people there were nice and friendly, especially when they discovered we were from New Zealand.

'Zat eez very, very far away' they would say, looking quite impressed. Then they would look at us kids, with their eyes narrowed, as if we were criminals and ask Mum, 'But why aren't zee children at school!?'

At least Mum thinks that's what they were saying. We kids relied on Mum's little bit of French that she had learnt for a year and half at Alliance Française in Wellington. She said she had a lot of knowledge in her head but a lot of difficulty getting words out of her mouth. She looked like a fish out of water sometimes; mouth open, gasping for air, and nothing coming out.

Chapter 6 But where are we going to live?

'Dearest,' said Dad casually to Mum on day three in France. 'I've just been in touch with Audrey, the PhD programme administrator at the university, and found out that there is an intensive mathematics course that I should have started *yesterday*. How would you feel if I was gone all day, every week-day, for two weeks?'

'Oh,' said Mum, so quietly that I could hardly hear her. She went from looking normal to miserable and glum, all in a nano-second.

Mum and Dad were expecting to have the first two weeks together in France to start finding their way around the city and doing important stuff. So I think it was a bit of a surprise for them when Dad was leaving the château early in the morning and coming back hot and sweaty in the evening, and just a bit tired out.

(Luckily for Dad his university programme was all in English because he knew even less French than Mum!)

And of course we had to find a house to live in, because we couldn't stay in James' apartment forever. One lunch time, Dad spoke to a couple of rental agents who knew some English, and who showed Dad three different houses. We chose the last one - the one we live in now, in the town of Ramonville St-Agne.

Ramonville St-Agne is pretty cool.

Mum and Dad had decided on this town on the outskirts of Toulouse because:

Number *ONE*: Ramonville St-Agne was on the metro Line B, the same metro line as Dad's university, so it was easy travelling for him (well, still 45 minutes each way, but not bad),

Number *TWO*: Mum didn't want to live smack-bang-in-the-middle-of-the-city-when-she-could-be-walking-on-the-grass-and-listening-to-the-birds-for-heaven's-sake, and

Number *THREE*: Mum and Dad thought a smaller town would have a nice community feel to it, lots of handy, local facilities, and it might be a bit easier to make friends.

And it did seem like an alright town to live in because at our house there would be a garden to play in, space to grow vegetables, and a driveway that we could zoom down on our bikes (when Dad finally bought some for us). We would also be able to watch these absolutely massive planes that looked like fat whales flying to the airport in Toulouse; they flew

31

right over our house. They were carrying enormous plane-parts from around Europe so that they could be put together and built into a real plane in Toulouse.

Mum had already seen this house on an accommodation website when we were still in New Zealand, and it was the one we chose! We probably wouldn't have had all that space in the city anyway.

Ramonville St-Agne is right next to the Canal du Midi which is this man-made (man-dug) river that was once used to transport goods on barges between Toulouse and the Mediterranean Sea. Now it transports tourists mostly on canal barges or other boats, while heaps of people walk, run and ride along the tow-path where the horses used to walk to pull the barges. It is lined on either side with big old trees (Mum says they are called *plane* trees) that sometimes droop down and even touch the water.

There are also big outdoor markets in Ramonville St-Agne twice a week (Wednesday and Saturday mornings) with lots of fruit and vegetables and cheese and meat and coffee and bread and flowers and bits and bobs of other things too. The *mairie* (the town council) shuts one whole street for the entire morning so that all the trucks and tables can be set up along the street under the trees (more big old plane trees).

I think lots of people just go to the markets to talk to their friends, and it takes ages to get anywhere if you go there on a Wednesday morning because there are so many people there, and because Mum wants to talk to everyone (or to *try* to anyway). But the fruit and vegetables are definitely cheaper, Mum says.

We found that the local library in Ramonville St-Agne, called *la médiathèque*, had ONE WHOLE SHELF of books written in English, including all the Harry Potter books, and it was really great to discover that little treasure trove. A library in France is usually called *la bibliothèque* but because this library had a big music section in it (called *la discothèque*!) the library became *la médiathèque*. Clear?! (Kind of?)

Next to the library we also found where the old men (and sometimes young men) played their games of *pétanque* – on the stony-sandy ground under the shade of the big, leafy plane trees. Pétanque is an old French game played with small but heavy balls, like bowling balls, but it's not really like bowling. There is a special throwing technique where you sometimes leap in the air a little bit and then try to throw your ball as close to the little marker ball as possible.

The old men are all very energetic and they wave their arms around and discuss the scores very loudly – like they are angry but they're not! They are having a really good time.

(You just can't stay watching them for very long because if you need the toilet you have to use the public one nearby. It is a *bit different* to what we are used to in New Zealand. (It's like a hole in the ground.) The first time Edward tried to use it he got 'wee-freeze'.)

People were really kind to us, giving us stuff that they didn't need any more. Olivia was really lucky because she was given some big boxes full of Barbie dolls and furniture and houses and cars. Well, it was lucky for her anyway. Definitely not something you would catch *me* playing with.

And we were given a car too. A *real* car (not a Barbie car). Awesome! A New Zealand family had been living in Toulouse and they were moving back to Auckland. They wanted to leave their car (a big Renault Espace) for us to use which was really nice of them. We were able to fit heaps of stuff into it, plus all of us.

However, it was *hyper-scary* driving on the WRONG SIDE OF THE ROAD in France, especially for the first time. Dad was driving, with all of us in the car, and heaps of our things, trying to work out the buttons and knobs and gears and stuff, while Mum kept directing us the wrong way because she couldn't understand the completely unfamiliar map. Dad had had a couple of practice runs in the car but he said it was different with all of us in the car with him.

'Mum and Dad, I have to tell you something,' I said that night as I went to bed. 'When we were all driving in the car for the first time I was even more nervous than when I was the lead actor in the school show at my old school! I was *really* worried that we were going to crash.'

And did you know that everything in the French cars is on the *other side of the car*? In New Zealand people drive on the left hand side of the road but the driver sits on the right hand side of the car. In France, they drive on the right hand side of the road, with the driver sitting on the left hand side of the car. It is completely reversed. Why, I ask you??

Dad said he kind of had to learn to drive all over again. He kept knocking his left hand on the side of the door as he went to change gear but there was no gear stick! Thankfully the pedals (accelerator, brake and clutch) were all in the same place!

Mum found she couldn't drive the big Renault Espace car without causing pain in her shoulder from an old injury. A friend very kindly found her a little British Rover car to drive, with the steering wheel on the NORMAL side of the car, so she was much happier after that.

Chapter 7 Meeting and greeting and organising and buying

'Bienvenue! Je m'appelle Marcel, et voici, ma femme, elle s'appelle Mélanie.'

Welcome! My name is Marcel and this is my wife, Mélanie.

The day we moved in to our house, our new French neighbours greeted us and immediately lent us some cups and plates and cutlery, so that we could eat and drink. Really nice! We only had our suitcases with us with our clothes and shoes and Dad's textbooks and stuff in them. The house was *completely empty* and it actually *ECHOED, Echoed, echoed* … when we spoke to each other.

There weren't any curtains or light shades either. And the kitchen only had the sink and some cupboards, so we had to buy a fridge, an oven, a table and some chairs, plus all the stuff you use in the kitchen, and of course beds and shelves and – *everything*. When we first moved in, we had to sleep on a pile of winter coats because us kids didn't have any beds (it was actually quite comfortable). Mum and Dad had an air bed to use – lucky them.

We did lots and lots and lots of trips to different shops and second hand stores to find stuff we needed. And *that* was a big adventure because we had to work out where to go and how to get there. It was all completely new. But we didn't buy a dishwasher straight away though because we had Mum.

We also met some other really friendly people, Susannah and Jack, who invited us for lunch not long after we arrived. Mum got in touch with Susannah by email when we were still in New Zealand (through friends-of-friends-of-friends, she said). They had two sons the same age as Edward and me, called Elliott and Pearce.

What was nice was that because they were from America they spoke English (a bit different to how we speak it but it was still English); so we could understand each other pretty well. Elliott (the boy my age) really liked the same sort of books as me, so we spent ages together, just reading, and playing with Lego. Edward and Pearce played together while Olivia brushed Susannah's hair. We saw them lots of times, which was great.

Susannah and Jack knew of some other people who were leaving Toulouse, and they arranged for us to have some of their old stuff like mats and baskets and pictures, and all sorts of funny things like a collection of heaps of unused soaps and shampoos from hotels they had stayed in. All those things made us feel like we were in a home again.

And it was definitely nice to be in *our own house* and to be together, just us. We moved in on the Saturday, after only two weeks staying at the château. On the last night at the château we had a farewell barbecue with lots of James' friends from university, and we ate barbecued duck hearts for the first time (salty and delicious). It started raining and we all had to run inside with our dinners.

Chapter 8 Doing important stuff like enrolling at school

On the Friday before we moved to our new house, Mum, Olivia, Edward and I visited the Secteur Education Jeunesse office (the education office for young people) in Ramonville St-Agne, to enrol us all for school. Mum and Dad had *promised* me that all Toulouse schools had a special programme to help non-French speaking kids like us learn French, and that was one reason I said that it *might* be okay to move to France.

Well, it was a bit of a shame really. Ramonville St-Agne was JUST OUTSIDE the Toulouse city limit, and so there was no special language integration programme here. We had already signed the agreement-thing for our house too so we couldn't change where we were going to live.

'Oh no! Disaster! Crisis alert! Certain doom!' I said, not very calmly.

Mum was like a stuck-record. She said that I was 'prone to exaggeration'. Like I always thought that something would be worse than it was.

'Mu-um, that's not true,' I said. 'I never, ever, *ever* exaggerate. EVER!'

'My point exactly, Matthew!' She just laughed.

So after lots of phone calls and waiting, the Secteur Education Jeunesse decided that we would be in the same class as the other kids our age at our local school, but we would go into the little kids' class (called CP) to learn French. I didn't like the sound of that one bit. I didn't expect to have to be sitting with the little kids when I was a big kid. That was going to be really bad for my credibility with the kids my age I reckoned, especially when I was trying to fit in and be normal.

But anyway, what could I do? Olivia and I were going to be starting at the École Élémentaire St Exupéry (the primary school) with Edward going to the next-door preschool, École Maternelle St Exupéry.

Okay, step one of trillions. Tick. Done.

That afternoon we went to meet *la directrice* (the headmistress), Madame Rousseau. She was really nice but didn't speak much English (and Mum didn't speak enough French).

'Oh, no,' said Mum anxiously. 'My beginner-level French isn't going to help me much this time!'

'Who's panicking now?' I said quietly to myself.

But suddenly this lady appeared to help us (an angel, Mum reckons). A French lady, Patricia, had lived in Wales with her Welsh husband, Dafydd, and she could speak English fluently, and she *just happened* to be visiting the school that afternoon. She translated everything for Mum. I could see Mum's face change from deeply worried to all bright and smiling. Madame Rousseau and Patricia were really friendly and welcoming, and they even showed Mum the stationery form, with a real live example so that she would know just what to buy.

Here are some of the French words on the stationery form: *un agenda* means a diary, *deux crayons* is two pencils and *une paire des ciseaux* is (can you guess?) a pair of scissors!

We then went to meet our new classes. Madame Rousseau was going to be my teacher for my class – CE2, and Madame Morel was Olivia's teacher for her class – CE1.

Boy was I freaking out. I smiled, even though I was really anxious.

I tried to see someone friendly in the room but all I could see was strange faces, and way too many of them. Everyone looked kind of excited to see us though, especially when Madame Rousseau showed the kids where New Zealand was on a world map.

She said, *'C'est très loin la Nouvelle Zélande! Très, très loin!'*

That means, 'It's a long way to New Zealand! A long, long way!' Boy, she was right about that!

But, hold on just a minute.

I actually WASN'T READY to start a new school. For a start, what on earth was anyone saying? And remember that I'm an I-like-to-know-what's-happening-at-every-moment-of-the-day kind of boy. I was feeling jumpy, jittery and really, really nervous.

Actually, Mum and Dad used to watch us especially carefully. Not to make sure we were up to no good this time, but desperately hoping that we were happy and not showing too many signs of 'bewilderment, despair and stress' at being flung to the other side of the world, Mum told me later.

Whenever we laughed I think she cried with relief.

Part II On being overwhelmed

Chapter 9 Starting our new school only two weeks after we arrived in France

In France, the first day back to school after the long summer holidays is a Really Big Deal. It's called *la rentrée*, (like 'the re-entry').

We were starting school two weeks after la rentrée which was a shame because I think it would have been good to do all that new stuff together with the other kids at school.

Strangely for me, I was about a quarter-excited to be going to a new school (but three-quarters scared) because I knew there would be some boys there I could play with and who might become my friends. I was missing my old friends in New Zealand though and I really needed some new ones. I didn't know how I was going to do that, you know, *make new friends*, when I couldn't speak to anyone, and they couldn't speak to me either.

I suppose I could have pretended I was Mr Bean. He's in a movie where he travels through France and can't understand a thing but he doesn't seem to mind at all. He can only say *oui* and *non* and *gracias* (yes and no in French, and thank you in Spanish) and that's it!

Well, that was just about the extent of my French too, only I didn't know *when* to say those words, and I really hoped that I wouldn't get into as much trouble as Mr Bean always seemed to.

So, we all arrived in the morning and Mum stayed with us for a while.

So far, I'm doing okay, I thought. I'm not *completely* flipping out, even though it feels like I've got a busy ant farm in my stomach, and I kind of feel like throwing up all the time.

'Bye kids. Be brave,' Mum said. 'Have a good day. See you in…*eight hours*.' She choked a bit and I thought she was going to cry.

I noticed that no other parents were waiting with their children; they all *bisous-ed* them goodbye at the gate, and then left.

'Huh? What's a bisou?' I imagine you might be asking yourself. Well it's a French thing. It's a kiss on each cheek to say hello, or goodbye. Actually it's more like a quick peck really and definitely not anything like a smoochey, lovey-dovey kiss. You don't do it to everyone, or all the time and the rules about when you do it can be a bit confusing.

Anyway, I went and hung around the edge of a basketball game just to watch it. I didn't really want to join in yet. I remember seeing one boy who came to school wearing an entire outfit of All Blacks rugby gear – cool! (The people here in Toulouse love rugby too, just like us.)

One thing that I did notice though was that being in a new place makes you become sort of *hyper-aware* of all the sights and smells and sounds and people and situations and feelings all around you. It's like your body is on full-danger-alert *all the time* and that you are waiting for an enemy attack at any moment, or something like that. But that could just be me, because you know Olivia seemed to find it okay.

And I was really aware that I was the new kid at the school and I didn't know a single person. The words of my parents kept jostling around in my mind. 'It's an adventure. It's a big, exciting family adventure,' I tried to tell myself.

But it didn't feel like an adventure to me though; more like stepping into space with no life-line, and about to run out of oxygen in my supply tank. H E L P!

Actually, one thing that helped a bit was that the kids all kind of looked like kids from New Zealand and they weren't dressed too differently to me or anything. I did notice that there were lots of North African kids who had skin that was browner than mine, and that lots of the boys had long hair. Olivia said she noticed that the girls were all quite little, and that she seemed to be one of the few kids with blonde hair.

Compared to New Zealand kids it seemed like some of the French kids needed just a bit of help with their teeth-brushing technique, as there were a few mucky, stained teeth about in the playground that I could see. Or, I wondered, maybe they didn't have toothbrushes in France, or perhaps they couldn't afford them? Or could it have had something to do with the sweets I saw lots of kids practically inhaling during the break times?

And then the day was over. I don't know what the heck happened all day at school because I was completely dazed. I hated not knowing the rules and not understanding what was being said. At one point I went into the little kids' class to try and learn French, but they were just babies (6 years old) and I was 8½ years old! It was outrageous! Olivia didn't seem to mind it so much because she was only one year older than them, and remember, Olivia loves everyone and everything.

Chapter 10 Meltdown – la première (the first)

But the second day of school was horrible. Honestly.

That morning when it was time to go to school, I started crying. Well it was more like blubbering and spluttering and sobbing and shouting really. I think I suddenly realised that this whole new school/new country/new language thing was WAY BIGGER THAN ME, and I couldn't cruise my way through it. I couldn't joke my way into favour with the kids, I couldn't play with them and show them my rugby cards from the cereal packets, I couldn't even ask them the way to the toilets!

Mum had bought lots of New Zealand stickers for us to give to the kids at our new school, but I didn't want to do that because I didn't know who the nice kids were.

I had made my mind up.

'I am NOT going back to that school!' I wailed. 'You can't make me! I don't like it! It's too hard! I'm staying at home!' I was deadly serious.

Dad had to leave to get to university so Mum was left with the three of us kids – all crying and wailing now. So Mum had to try everything and anything she could think of to get me into the car.

'Darling Matthew, we all knew it would be hard to start with, but it *will* get better,' she coaxed.

'You've got to be patient, give it time, things will work out,' she wheedled.

'You can do it Matthew; you're a big, clever, likeable boy,' she buoyed.

'Come on, Matthew. Come! On! Just get in the [unrepeatable word] car!' She was getting quite fed up with me now. She was ready to tug me by the ear, or maybe even drop me off at someone else's house for the rest of my life.

Mum and Dad had both started new schools when they were little too. Mum said to me later that she knew how hard it was, but she also knew that I wouldn't advance or progress if I didn't try! She was being tough to me to be kind to me, or so she said.

(But I do have to point out that Mum didn't start school in *another country*, now did she?!)

Despite her kind-toughness, I stood firm.

'No, Mum. You can't make me go back there. I won't do it!'

I can be very stubborn when I am upset.

'Alright darling, I understand,' she said to me, rather surprisingly, suddenly changing tack.

'How about a little drink of special juice? You know the juice we only have at dinner time? Perhaps a little drink might help you calm down? I'll get it for you.'

She poured the drink and handed it to me saying, 'Sometimes you just need to do something a little bit different when you are upset, just to take your mind off…'

Well I was *not* going to go along with that little game. All I wanted to do was yell and shout, so I threw my head back and wrenched away from Mum. Juice went splattering all over my face, hair and clothes, and all over Mum too.

'Yaaargh! Gross!' I screamed, completely outraged and quite annoyed at myself.

But the funny thing was, it was kind of like giving a person with the hiccups a big fright: suddenly they don't have hiccups any more. Well, this had the same effect on me and it distracted me from my hyper-out-of-control state so that all I wanted to do was get that juice off me. I did *not* want to smell like passion fruit and mango all day, that's for sure.

We cleaned me up and Mum got changed too. Then we all clambered into the car, and drove to school. I was calmer and more subdued, even though now I was a bit worried about being late.

'Okay Mum,' I said, realising with quiet doom that I couldn't get out of this terrible situation. 'I'll try *one* more day…'

In the meantime, Olivia had started and then stopped her crying. She had had a group of girls gather around her on her first day, so she was feeling a bit better about it all than me. Edward was starting his school in a couple of days' time so he had a bit more time with Mum at home (lucky boy). When he was crying, he was crying with me out of sympathy I reckon.

Chapter 11 The first days at school

After a few days, I started making some friends. Ha! Yeah right! I *wish*!

Some of the kids did try to include me but I couldn't join in with their conversations though and that made me feel really stink. It was really weird hearing a new language for the first time too. It sounded like this continuous stream of, like, nonsense baby sounds all joined together. You couldn't tell where one sound or word stops and the next starts. It seemed like a miracle to me that anyone could understand a thing!

How the heck can anyone even *start* to understand that? I wondered desperately. I was really aware that I was out of my depth and treading pretty deep waters.

Someone had said to our family before we came to France that 'play is a universal language', and that us kids would have no problem at school. Well, they were kind of right. When a ball appeared, everyone knew to kick it around to each other; we didn't have to discuss the rules to know how to kick a ball around or anything. I could join in with that. And I liked that *les animateurs* tried to involve me in their games though – basketball and stuff – just so that I had something to do, but I didn't really like basketball.

But wait a minute, what on earth are *les animateurs*? I hear you ask.

The first cool thing I noticed at school was that they have these guys and girls in the school (in their early twenties I think) who run a before-, during- and after-school care programme called CLAE (pronounced *claiye*). They are there during the school day and play with us kids a lot.

Personally, I think most of them are chosen for their ability to SHOUT LOUDLY ACROSS THE PLAYGROUND because they are really, really, awesomely good at shouting; including the girl animateurs, which I thought was pretty darned impressive.

The days at school were really, really long though (from 9.00 am to 5.00 pm), and we had to eat in the canteen with the other kids at lunchtime. Mum thought that was excellent because we would get to try lots of different French food (and she wouldn't have to make our lunches every day like she did in New Zealand). We got two hours for our lunch break: one hour to sit down and eat our three course meal, and the other hour to go and play.

I was so grumpy and tired when I got home.

And all that newness was completely mucking up my balanced life of liking-to-know-what's-what and what's-going-to-happen-next. I was crying a lot at home and was quite snappy at everyone. I also used to read and read and read my books in English that we had brought over from New Zealand (Bear Grylls, Zac Power, Harry Potter, Percy Jackson, Captain Underpants) because at least that was something I could do well. I used to be a really clever kid, and now I felt like I was the dumbest in the class.

Actually, sometimes I don't even think my nice teacher knew what to do with me. I wouldn't speak. Well, to tell you the truth, I wouldn't even *try* to speak because I was scared of being laughed at. The kids really did laugh at me sometimes and it put me off trying.

'But Mum, I *am* trying to be brave. It's just really hard,' I told her at night.

And then this terrible thing happened. I think Mum and Dad had mentioned it, and I had seen it happen, but I was not prepared for it to happen to me. Some of the French girls at school wanted to *bisou* ME! It was all very well for their parents to bisou them, but not me! Oh no! I complained several times to my Dad that the girls just wanted to kiss me.

'How do you say in French – stop kissing me now; I don't like it!' I begged Dad to tell me. He laughed and said something like 'Son, you're a bit too young to appreciate it now, but one day you'll love it.'

Gross! I thought Dads and sons were supposed to be on the same team!

While we're on the subject of Dad I'll tell you a bit about what he was up to. He was the oldest in his class at the Toulouse School of Economics (University of Toulouse 1-Capitole, apparently). Most of the students were quite young, while Dad was the only one that year who had three children and lots of grey in his beard. He started to dress like a student too; jeans every day, t-shirt, and canvas sneakers. Mum got a bit worried about him because she was used to seeing him all smart and handsome in a suit.

He even got a French haircut. Well, he asked the hairdresser to cut his hair in a style *comme un français* (like a French man). Luckily the hairdresser understood his French.

He was especially busy for the first term at university, but we thought it would get better and a bit quieter after that.

Nope.

The second and third terms were even busier, and I think Mum forgot what Dad looked like a bit. After dinner and after helping to get us to bed at night, he would study through the evening until after midnight, so that he could at least spend the weekends with us.

Chapter 12 Living in a daze

'WILL YOU CHILDREN STOP TALKING AND LISTEN TO ME, NOW?!'

Here's the thing: you know how I said that the animateurs can shout? Well some of the teachers here CAN SHOUT REALLY LOUDLY TOO! At least, they seem to shout more than we are used to anyway. In New Zealand, shouting is kind of 'fighting talk' whereas here it seems more normal to have a bit of a shout.

Dad thinks it is the 'passionate, expressive, Mediterranean temperaments' of the French people. I think it's just because they like it, or maybe someone once told them they had a good shouting voice. But once they've had their little shout, they are nice again.

You have to be really polite and respectful to the teachers too. Better make sure you look them in the eye and say *bonjour* (hello) every day. Don't forget!

So that was one big difference about France, and one reason that I found it really hard in the little kids' classroom trying to learn French. The teacher

SHOUTED way more than I was used to. Well, it was mostly when kids were doing something wrong, but I was used to the gentle, hushed concentration of learning (and frighteningly calm and quiet telling-offs) in my Montessori classroom in New Zealand, and this was *massively* different.

We didn't call our teachers by their first name either, like we do in New Zealand. It was either *maître* (master) for the men or *maîtresse* (mistress) for the women. Mum said that we stopped that sort of thing in New Zealand about 50 years ago but she said that she thought it was good to be so polite.

I still went to my usual class every day (CE2), and sat and listened. I started recognising some of the words, like *oui* and *non*, but the teacher spoke so fast it was almost impossible to even hear those words at times. I felt so stupid. I had a French/English dictionary on my desk and I would sometimes look up a word or use the computer to check a translation of something or other. I did recognise my name though, but it sounded a bit different when my teacher said it, like *'Mah-tew'*.

Actually, my parents did send me and my sister to an hour's French lesson at Alliance Française each week when we were still in New Zealand. It is an international French language teaching place and there was one in Wellington. We went there on the bus on Thursdays after school. Edward was too little to go but Mum and Dad thought it would give us older kids a bit of French to use when we finally arrived in France, and at least make us familiar with some French sounds. I don't know if it helped me much because I didn't seem to remember stuff from one week to the next (except maybe *bonjour*, *au revoir* and *bonne nuit*). Olivia could remember more than I could.

I do remember playing some fun games there though, and drinking juice and eating half-moon-shaped pastries called *croissants* and hiding under tables while Eloise, our teacher, called out French names or colours or something. I just liked eating the croissants.

And Mum used to play some French CD on the car stereo whenever we drove anywhere in Wellington. She was learning French then too, and someone clever had told her that you can learn a lot by singing along to songs in another language. It didn't work for me, that's for sure.

Mum only learnt the words in the songs that were in English. Ha!

But here in France at school it seemed like most of the time I spent my time drawing complicated pictures of suspended aerial road systems or I read my Harry Potter book in English, which didn't feel like learning French to me. The teacher was really busy with lots of things and she couldn't concentrate on me all the time.

I used to get sort of angry at times, and would sometimes have quite an impressive temper tantrum. I even surprised myself.

Once when we were walking home from school, I stubbed my toe a bit. I wanted Mum to stop and look after me, but she had to rush home with Edward (because he REALLY had to go to the toilet, like RIGHT NOW!). I was über-mad with her.

'You NEVER help me when I need you to! You are ALWAYS helping the other kids. You ignore me! You don't love me! In fact, YOU DON'T EVEN WANT ME IN THIS FAMILY!' I shouted at her loudly down the street. I can shout loudly too, you know!

And to punish her for being so mean, I hid. I hid for one whole hour in some really overgrown bushes by the side of the road. Mum started to get a bit worried about me, and she, Olivia and Edward came up the street to try and find me. They were calling out to me and I could see and hear them but because I was still so mad, I kept really quiet. Angrily, stubbornly quiet…

'Matthew, I know you can hear me.' She was bluffing. She, Olivia and Edward called out for me for ages. Then Mum said, 'We are going to start dinner soon. Come home when you are ready.'

Well, after another half an hour I got a bit sick of that and I was getting quite hungry too. So I went home and just kind of walked in the door like I had arrived home as normal, as if I was Dad walking in the door after a long day at university.

'Hi Mum,' I said.

I think I gave Mum a bit of a fright but she didn't show it too much.

'Oh, hi Matthew,' she answered calmly.

Hmmmm, I thought to myself; that was just a bit *too* calm for Mum.

After dinner, she and I had a bit of a chat.

'Matthew, my sweetness and most precious treasure,' she said in that way of hers. 'I understand that you are getting frustrated with all sorts of things right now, but I would appreciate if you could hide in your room next time, rather than up the street. At least I will know where you are when you are hiding.'

That kind of didn't make sense, but I was a bit too close to tears to say anything.

Then she gave me a big hug and told me she loved me, and that she was really proud of me.

'I love you too, Mum,' I said, not wanting to let her go for a while.

Later in the month we had a sports day of running races with all the other schools in the area. We had to run for what seemed like forever. It was dreadful. I came second to last, just in front of the boy who had a sore leg. Oh man! (Actually, I think that boy did really well to even finish the race.)

My credibility was even more shattered. And I was so puffed I could hardly breathe properly, let alone talk. Didn't they know I was much better at sprint races and not these endless round the track, up the hill, along the path, by the river, under the trees, and around again races??

'Come on Matthew, you can do it!' shouted Mum, as she ran up the last stretch with me.

Most of those French boys just ran like the wind, but I didn't even know how far I had to go, of course, because I didn't know the rules. Afterwards, I couldn't talk for ages afterwards, and I hurt all over.

'Mum,' I explained later on, 'I would have done much better if I had known how far I had to run, but I didn't understand what the guy was saying before the race. He was speaking that crazy French language again!'

I felt really bad about that. If I had been able to ride my bike I would have beaten them all!

Chapter 13 The first term at school, trying to learn French

One day Mum was chatting with the kind French lady (the angel), Patricia, whom we had met before.

'Patricia, do you know if there is anything I can do to help the children with their French, and settling in? They are all having a hard time, but particularly Matthew. They could all do with some help.'

And wouldn't you know it, but Patricia *just happened* to be a teacher who goes around different schools helping kids with any difficulties. So after the first term of complete confusion, Olivia and I started seeing Patricia once a week, last thing on a Friday afternoon.

But I hated it. Doom and gloom for me again, and I could *not* see the light-at-the-end-of-the-tunnel that Dad kept talking about.

'Mum,' I declared angrily one day after school, 'I know that I'm not allowed to say 'stupid' but this thing I have to do with Patricia is stupid. I don't understand anything, and the more she talks to me in

French, the less I understand. I am not learning anything.'

Patricia kept trying to play games with me, and of course she only spoke French with me. She kept asking me questions like I understood what she was saying. She just didn't seem to understand that I didn't understand (or perhaps she thought I would *suddenly* understand?).

Olivia, for some unknown reason, *could* understand some of the words and sentences, while I could only hear gabbling. How on earth did she do it?? Once more I told Mum, 'I am not going to do that again!' hoping that this time she would listen.

'I really don't want to be in France. It was so much easier in New Zealand with all my friends. I really miss being a clever boy. Here, everyone thinks I'm a dimwit! I hate it!'

Of course, Mum made me go there a few more times. I got a real surprise though, when after a while, even Patricia *agreed* that it really wasn't working with me, and I stopped having to go! Amazing!

'Madame Meade,' she said on the phone one day to Mum. 'I 'ave tried my 'ardest wiz Matthew, but 'e does not seem to want to learn. 'E does not try; 'e does not even speak to me. 'E 'as put up a big barrier between us and I do not know 'ow to remove eet.'

Yep, I thought, she's got that right. Now I thought I was going to have it easy, not seeing

Patricia any more. She was really nice, but I didn't think I was getting anywhere much, that's for sure.

But one day Mum had other ideas.

'Oh man! Not another 'good idea' Mum!' I complained.

Mum made me try this school support programme run in Ramonville St-Agne, especially for kids who need help with their homework. I went there about three times.

On the second visit, the really nice lady who was supposed to help me couldn't make it, so this other volunteer lady offered to help me. I don't know what she was expecting of me, but I got so annoyed with her I was ready to run out of the room.

'This is exactly what doesn't help me, Mum,' I protested, trying to explain it to Mum, who was there with me hovering in the background. 'This lady expects me to know stuff I haven't been taught and this is *not* helping me to learn!'

I was so mad. And then I started to cry, even though they were trying to distract me by offering me little cakes to eat. Under most normal circumstances, that would have worked wonderfully. But not that day.

Everything in the French language is based around learning your verbs (your 'doing' words, like running, walking, eating, coughing, sneezing, etc) and how the endings of the verbs change depending on who is doing the doing-thing, and when.

Thinking about this a bit later (now that I'm older), I reckon this volunteer helper lady might have been a bit angry with me because I didn't know my verbs and what to do with them and stuff like that. Maybe she had never met anyone like me before who hadn't been speaking French for ages. Maybe she didn't realise that I had come from another country, far, far away. A country where we learn our language in a completely different way.

'What *is* a verb, anyway?!' I cried helplessly.

Chapter 14 And why the heck didn't I go to an English-speaking school in France instead of being totally immersed into a French school and forced against my will to learn another language?!

And then I was *so mad* with my parents when I found out that I could have gone to an international school where everything was taught in English. I could even have gone to a bi-lingual Montessori school in Labège (pronounced *lah-beige*), not far from Ramonville St-Agne, where they spoke half English-half French! Why the heck wasn't *that* happening?!

Well, those schools were *really* expensive. Most of the kids who went there had all their fees paid by the company their parents were working for ('expat' or 'expatriate' families), or else they were really rich, or else the parents didn't want their children to lose their English language, or for heaps of other reasons.

'Our situation is a bit different, Matthew my sweet,' said Mum one day. 'Dad is a student right now so, unfortunately, we won't be able to afford the fees.'

Oh COME ON! I thought. What kind of reason is that? This is *so unfair*!

But more importantly, Mum and Dad said that they also really wanted us all to have a 'genuine French experience' and not stick to knowing people who only spoke English. Even though none of us spoke French very well, Mum and Dad reckoned that 'total immersion' (which kind of means 'throwing-us-in-the-deep-end-of-the-swimming-pool-and-forcing-us-to-learn-to-swim-the-hard-way') would be a quick and efficient way of learning the language, although it might just be a little bit painful *in the beginning…*

'If we are going to be in France, we want to have as rich an experience as we can. That means learning French, and living and mixing with French people. It'll be great!' they would say really reassuringly, trying to jolly us along.

'And if we live where all the expatriate-English-speaking-people live, we won't have the chance of getting to know so many French people. That would be a bit of a shame.'

Before we came to France, Mum and Dad spoke to some people who had lived in France for 15 months with their teenage children. They were very helpful, for Mum and Dad anyway.

'Kids who go to English-speaking schools in France can sometimes end up a bit confused about where they are,' they explained. 'Are we in France? Or are we in the country of our native language – England or America or New Zealand, etc? Which country or language should we be concentrating on, and why?'

They continued. 'Having seen our own children adapt so well to the French school system, we think that total immersion is an option really worth considering. It will be jolly hard to start with, but the children are young. Now is the perfect time for them. And it won't prolong the agony of learning a new language. In fact, once our daughter took a book with her on a holiday we had in France, and she was thoroughly enjoying reading it. She was half way through it before she realised it was in French. And this was about seven months into our time in France. If she can do it, your kids certainly can too!

'Yes, total immersion in a French school is definitely an option worth thinking about.'

Chapter 15 How was Olivia doing?

Well, Olivia is really arty and so she really enjoyed learning to write in the 'cursive' style (old-fashioned swirly writing where the letters join up like your grandmother used to do and that almost everyone here in France still does, except me).

She spent ages just copying stuff down – her name mostly. She really loves dancing too, by the way, but she didn't do that at school.

And, she's got this really musical ear Mum says (although it looks quite normal to me), and she likes to sing and whistle. She's always humming something or other. Dad reckons that when the French people speak it's a bit like they are singing, so I guess Olivia picked up on that a bit too.

There are some experts somewhere who say that it's easier for kids to pick up a new language *before* they turn eight years old. Doh! for me. But for Olivia and Edward it was a good time.

Olivia drew lots of pictures in class, and listened a lot. She was quite quiet, even though the other girls looked after her nicely and didn't laugh at her, but she did seem to learn stuff more quickly than me. She wasn't at the same level at school as me, so she wasn't expected to know a whole heap of stuff already (like I was).

Sometimes she cried a bit at night though, and a few times she even got really, really angry and would shout and scream and throw things around her room!

'Yaaargh!' she would scream and shout. 'I don't like you Mum! I don't like you Dad! LEAVE…ME…ALONE!'

She was like a wild animal.

Even though she's quite a nice girl, she can drop down into these dark, dark moods that you can't even tickle her out of.

When she was little, she even scratched into her desk at home, *'I dont lik you anymor Mum'* and then she signed it *'from Matt'*, like I had done it! That was terrible!

And Dad said that sometimes Olivia's face would go 'dark', like these massive storm clouds were descending, and we would just have to wait for her to come out of it – we couldn't jolly her along, *not at all*.

With me, if I was in a grumpy mood, Mum and Dad just used to say 'Don't smile, Matthew!' and suddenly I was giggling and rolling around the floor, trying not to pee in my pants. Or worse, Dad would break out his secret weapon and become *the tickle monster* and tickle me mercilessly until I gave in and smiled.

Anyway, in France Mum starting letting Olivia come home for lunch so that she could have a break from school. She had to go back to school after lunch though. She found the canteen a bit noisy, and at times she just wanted to be quiet.

Poor Olivia started getting migraines too, which made her feel really bad until she vomited and then she felt a bit better. And the hot weather even made her get these really impressive bleeding noses sometimes.

Once Dad got a telephone call to come and pick Olivia up from school because she had 'blood on her knees'. At least, that's what he *thought* the teacher said (he was using a mixture of English and French), but what he actually said was, 'Olivia has blood on her *nez'*, which is the French word for nose. She had a bleeding nose!

Olivia and I both found mathematics easier to pick up than French – probably because the numbers were the same, even if the names for them were different. It was a relief to find *something* that I could kind of understand. It was much easier to learn the names of the numbers, than all the new vocabulary, grammar rules and verb endings! And even Dad, with his bad French, could help me with the maths.

Actually, once we knew the numbers we could work out the time. The French people use the 24 hour clock which is fine up until midday. After that if it's 1.00 pm you write 13h00, 4.00 pm is 16h00, and then 8.30 pm is 20h30, and so on like that.

Yay! I could get *that*.

When Olivia had her seventh birthday party in December she invited a lot of little French girls over. They mostly did drawings to start with. Their names were Ludivine, Lola, Celine, Brigitte, Alicia, and Gabrielle. I heard Olivia trying to speak in French to them which I thought was incredible. Mum and Dad were pretty impressed too, they said.

She was a bit sad after the party though. Apparently, once some of the girls found her stash of Barbie dolls, they enjoyed them too much to play pass-the-parcel or musical-statues. They had probably never seen so many Barbie dolls in one place before.

I think Olivia really wanted to see her New Zealand friends, right *then*.

Chapter 16 And what about Edward?

Edward, in maternelle, mostly followed the other kids around, played running races and made funny sounds, which didn't really need anyone to talk much in French.

Mum said it was fun to watch the little kids playing together. She said they kind of followed a silent instruction of what to do and where to move to next, like those fish that swim in groups in the ocean and create those fantastic shapes and move in completely random directions. Edward just became like one of those fish, and he moved around with the other kids.

He wore his All Blacks cap a lot, and the other kids sure liked that.

He kept complaining about the noise though. He seemed to really worry about the kids screaming and shouting outside at playtimes, and sometimes he came home with a sore head.

And there was one little girl, Sophie, who just wanted to give him kisses and cuddles too, because she might have thought he was a bit lonely.

Edward's teacher, Madame Titine and her teaching assistant, Marie-Blanche, were really kind, and spoke just a little bit of English. Madame Titine told Mum that school wasn't obligatory until a child was six years old, so to start with Edward was only going for half days. (Lucky, lucky, lucky him.)

Madame Titine suggested to Mum that Edward could join them on a school trip to the zoo. I think he started feeling happier with the other kids after that because he knew them a bit better. Mum went on the trip too. All Mum could say to the kids on the trip though was 'Attention!' and 'Stop!' only with a French accent, but she did learn some of the French names of the animals, like zebra is *zèbre*, tiger is *tigre*, hippopotamus is *hippopotame*.

After a while Edward started staying for lunch and eating the canteen food. Actually he was enjoying school more when Mum started leaving him there for the whole day. Weird. Marie-Blanche always sat with him in the canteen and encouraged him to try *just a little bit* of something he didn't know. He eats tons of stuff now.

'Yummy, yummy. Beetroot,' he will say, or 'Goody, it's white asparagus and vinaigrette today!' or 'Oh Mum, they had tomatoes in the canteen today. I *love* tomatoes!' (He's not like me, at all.)

Throughout the first term though, Madame Titine would often greet Mum at the end of the day with a sad look on her face, shaking her head, and shrugging her shoulders.

'Ah, Madame Meade. *Aïe, aïe, aïe!* Eet eez very difficult you know, eet eez *très difficile*, trying to explain zings to Edward. 'e doesn't understand us and we don't understand 'im. *Ah, oui, c'est très, très difficile.*'

'I know, Madame, it *is* difficult,' Mum would sympathise, 'but each day Edward will be learning a bit more and his comprehension will increase. Just keep trying! You can do it! *Bonne chance! Bon courage!*'

Good luck! Have courage!

We knew it was hard – for everyone! And the teachers didn't have any extra resources to help Edward (or me and Olivia) to learn French.

They were mostly used to kids who had been speaking French from the day they gurgled their first French gurgle as a baby, or said *maman* (mummy) or *baguette* (a long stick of bread) as a little kid.

And they didn't have access to help, any more than we did - *aïe, aïe, aïe* was right! And they certainly hadn't seen any New Zealand kids in their school before.

One Sunday we went on a let's-have-an-explore-trip to a city near Toulouse called Albi (pronounced *al-bee*). It was the first time we had driven out of Toulouse so it was really interesting looking at the different countryside. I noticed that there weren't

77

many animals (cows and sheep) like we were used to in New Zealand; rather absolutely gigantic open fields with lots of crops or something growing in them.

Albi was quite interesting and old.

It had a totally massively big cathedral in the centre of the old city which was made out of brick. It had amazingly 'elaborate' (Mum said) carvings and paintings inside. Some of it was a bit gruesome though - about 'hell, death and damnation' which was not very nice for us to look at, and I think Edward got a bit scared so we went outside.

And that's when Edward noticed how MASSIVE the cathedral was. He was very, very impressed by this, and he talked about it a lot. Later, he tried hard to explain to our Swedish friend, Elisabeth, how big it was.

'Elisabeth, that cathedral was *so* big. You should have seen it!' said Edward excitedly.

'Really?' said Elisabeth. 'How big was it?'

'Oh, it was *enormous*. Actually, it was bigger than…(thinking hard)…my *WHOLE BODY*!'

We went to a place called Foix too (pronounced *fwah*). It has a big castle on top of the hill in the centre of town and we climbed all the way up there. It was our first big trip on the *péage* (big toll road).

You can drive up to 130 kilometres/hour on it! That's over 80 miles per hour! And it didn't us take long to get there, at all.

We climbed up a hill to another castle (some of it in ruins) but we could see great views of the town and hills all around.

It was cool (and cold)!

Chapter 17 Three months later – were my troubles over yet?

We were doing okay – just – but all of us kids did get kind of sick though – me with sick stomachs and a cough, Olivia with horrible warts on her feet, and Edward with nasty spots on his body. Sounds so gross! Dad thinks it was because we were all coping with lots of changes.

Mum had to take us to various medical people and try to be understood. She said she was really looking forward to the day when us kids would be able to translate for her. 'Yeah right, I thought, like that's ever gonna happen' – in the words of my good-friend-and-green-hero, SHREK.

In the end, poor Edward had to see a specialist to help him get rid of his spots. And my sore tummy and coughs meant that I had quite a few days off school (even though I seemed to suddenly get much better by around mid-morning).

And as for me, after three months I was definitely a bit happier than when I first started school.

I wasn't picking on Edward so much, or saying so many mean things to Olivia. Mum said I was more helpful, and we started earning some pocket money by doing jobs around the house, which meant that I could buy more Lego.

And it was good getting out and about and seeing different stuff around Toulouse and in the countryside.

We had a bit of a reward system too. If we showed that we were trying hard at school, we would get a gift of some particular thing we really wanted (Lego and a skateboard for me). Also, we had a toy-fund from all the toys we sold in New Zealand so we were allowed to choose one or two things from the shops *occasionally*.

I also met some kids from the neighbourhood and got to play with them a bit. A girl from my class, Lilou, used to visit us a lot too. She just used to smile a lot at me, and I really hoped she didn't want to kiss me as well. Oh man!

Dad was still studying really hard during the week, and we didn't see him that much without a large textbook close by. I really missed him, but we saw him at breakfast, dinner, at bedtime, and in the weekends.

One day Mum came back from Toulouse city chuckling to herself. That day, three different French people had stopped her and asked her for directions. They thought she was a local French person!

She didn't know what to say back to them though, so she just blushed and giggled and tried to remember how to say in French, 'I'm sorry but I don't speak French.' I reckon those people must have found that quite confusing because it would have been like me saying, 'I don't speak English' – *in English.*

I made it to the end of the second term. And then it snowed! We had a great time freezing our butts off and throwing snowballs at Dad. He had to go to an exam one morning when it was snowing and all the trains and buses had stopped. He got there late, to find that the course professor was stuck in the snow somewhere, so there was no exam; well, it was postponed anyway.

It snowed about three or four times in the first year. We had never really been in the snow much before and it was heaps of fun. I don't think my hands have ever been so cold in my life because I didn't really know then that gloves were a good idea. Sometimes when it snowed, it meant that we couldn't get to school because we didn't have shoes that wouldn't slip and slide all over the place. And it was too dangerous to drive.

Once Mum tried to drive us to school in the car and only got half-way before there were lots of cars stopped behind a van that couldn't drive up an icy hill. We had to walk the rest of the way to school, and try not to fall over.

We could also see a road from our kitchen window so on other snowy mornings we could watch cars sliding into each other with a bit of a bang and a crash. They weren't going very fast though, so no one died or was hurt (and there was no blood, thank goodness).

Chapter 18 A few things we saw and did

Well, we started doing a few trips and visits and getting out to explore things around us a bit more.

In December we went to a Swedish Festival of Lights party, called 'Sankta Lucia' with our new Swedish-French friends, Henri and Julie, and their children Sophie and Tobi. The kids were at school with us and lived on the same street. I had never been to this Lucia thing before and I have to say that it's a very bizarre festival.

There was one girl who stood incredibly still like a statue, with burning candles sitting on a frame on her head, for about 45 minutes, while the choir sang these Christmasey songs. Some of the little girls wore the candles on their heads too (pretend candles) and they carefully held real candles.

Our friend, Sophie, fainted during the show (she was one of the singers), and she had to go to hospital because she cut her head a bit and needed some stitches (yes, there was some blood and I could hardly eat my Swedish treats later). She was okay though.

Mum and Dad enjoyed the party and they drank spicy Swedish mulled wine, called *glögg*. The Swedish people at the festival were really kind and friendly and their English was unbelievably good, like they had been speaking English from when they were born. I heard them *speak* some Swedish too (apart from the Swedish they sang in the songs) and it sounded as if their mouths were full of soup. It was strange!

In Toulouse there is something called Cité de l'Espace which is this great big place that has lots of different and exciting things for kids to see and do, and it's all about SPACE! There are heaps of industries and agencies and organisations in Toulouse that work on space stuff. (Just quietly, I think it might be SPY stuff!)

It was awesome. I drove this cool moon buggy bike thing, and then I jumped and bounced around on a moon-walking simulation machine thing that got strapped around my body.

I even had a look through the inside of a real space station (well, it was a copy of one that used to be up in space anyway), and that now has people happily strolling through it. That was cool!

We saw this awesome 3D show about space, and there was also a movie that was above us and below us and all around us in a big dome, all about the creation of the universe and time and deep space (Mum *really* liked that). I liked the movies showing early rockets falling over, or flying out of control and then exploding into great balls of fire – no one was in them so Mum didn't mind me watching them.

It was really great doing these fun, different things because it really took my mind off how hard school was. We had two visitors from New Zealand to stay with us – Aunty Angela, and our friend Katherine – and it was actually quite nice to see some people who we had known for more than *just a few weeks*.

And once when we all needed a break from studying and stressing, we went on a get-out-of-Toulouse-quick-and-enjoy-a-change-of-scenery-trip to a little village on the Mediterranean coast called Collioure (pronounced *kol-lee-ure*). I really liked it there.

It was really great to play on the beach and sort through all the different coloured stones. We brought back heaps of them in the car with us. Edward really enjoyed it too, that is until he fell into the water that he had been watching closely as it was lapping over some steps leading down into the sea. All of a sudden he *completely lost his balance* and fell forward, face down, like a starfish. It was really cold water, and he cried a lot. Poor old Edward.

And I've got an image in my mind from that time that just won't go away. Mum, me, Olivia and Edward were in the car waiting at some traffic lights one day. We were on our way to pick up our other

Swedish friend, Elisabeth, from the metro station (she's really nice and does things like baking with us. Alright!).

This teenage boy with the typical long, floppy hair, skinny, drain-pipe jeans hanging off his *derrière* (backside), with an ipod in his ears was crossing the road at the lights in front of us. There were a few giggly teenage girls walking behind him and suddenly we heard them screeching and screaming like I'd never heard before. The boy's drain-pipe jeans had just completely dropped down around his ankles! We thought he would stop to pull them up but he DIDN'T! He just kept walking like nothing had happened.

I noticed that he had a bit of a smile on his face; probably because the girls could see his flash undies, and he was probably quite pleased to be noticed because that's what teenage boys are like from what I've heard. He was really showing off. I don't think I'll be like that though. If it was me, I would *definitely* stop and pull up my jeans!

But, anyway, I reckon the best trip we did in the first few months was to this place called Carcassonne (pronounced *kar-kah-sonne*). It's about an hour's drive from Toulouse. I didn't know what to expect but Dad had seen this place when he had passed by on a train a few years ago, and he wanted to come back and visit it with all of us.

It's amazing! It's even a world-heritage site, which means it's kind of protected for all the world to see, and so that it won't fall down in a hurry.

It's this really, really big, old walled city and it looks like you've stepped into another world – *a magic world!*

There are two walls that are really thick and built massively strongly, and there are lots and lots of long thin windows set into the outside wall from where you can fire your arrows at the enemy who might be trying to attack the city.

There's a château and cathedral inside the walls too – where all the people who were liked by the local ruler lived and worked in the olden days.

Even now there are still people who live there but I think it's the people who own the tourist shops and run the restaurants.

And I suppose I should mention that I was in a nativity play before Christmas, too.

My character was a grumpy innkeeper and I said a line or two, quite dramatically.

In fact I was really convincingly, *genuinely* grumpy, mostly because I fancy myself more as a famous BMX competitor than an actor, and I wasn't too happy about being in that play. Olivia was an angel, *of course.*

Edward was an assistant shepherd with a toy sheep, and he just followed the big shepherds around.

Chapter 19 Santa Claus finds France

I was really pleased that Santa Claus had got our new address in France because on Christmas morning there were lots of presents under our real tree.

(And just so that you know – *I don't believe in Santa Claus*. I know it's just your Mum and Dad, but if it means getting more Lego I will *definitely* play their little game – hee hee!.

We had a bit of a quiet day. It wasn't like in New Zealand where we would usually be at Granna and Grandpa's house and we'd play with our new toys and read books and eat all day.

We made lots of phone calls to New Zealand even though they had already had all of their Christmas day because of the time difference between the northern and southern hemispheres.

It was weird thinking about the difference in time between Europe and Oceania; when it's night in France, it's day in New Zealand, just like how the seasons are opposite too. Bizarre.

And here are some differences about Christmas in France, things that we weren't used to. It's cold and it gets dark early, and it might even snow, you don't have barbecues and there's not heaps of fresh strawberries to eat. Instead, you stay inside, keep warm and think about your family in New Zealand who had Christmas 12 hours earlier, probably on a beach or in a garden with lots of sun, and with yummy food, like a barbecue and salads for lunch and an enormous pavlova (meringue) and whipped cream for dessert, with a long game of cricket or badminton on the back lawn later in the afternoon when the food was gone and the grown ups were all asleep.

S T O P I T!

Part III On progressing nowhere

Chapter 20 Oh man, back to school again

During the holidays we mostly just hung out at home. It had been really great to turn our backs on school for two weeks during the Christmas holidays and to eat yummy roast lamb from New Zealand (we found some in the local supermarket!).

I also had a couple of visits to friends' houses (French friends!) and a sleepover at another friend's house.

Then one day, 'Mum, Mum, Mum!' I shouted excitedly. 'I've got THREE birthday invitations!' I was really happy to see my friends again when school started, and boy, those invitations made me feel great!

French kids' birthday parties are pretty much like normal birthday parties that I used to go to in New Zealand. Lots of kids come around to visit; or you go to a special adventure/bouncy/park/activity place some-where; there are lots of presents that the kids rip right into; maybe some games; and definitely stacks of party food and sweets. You don't seem to give the party girl or boy a birthday card though. That's a bit different.

Parents don't usually stay at French parties, even for the little kids' parties. They are also mostly held on a Saturday or Sunday from about 3.00 pm (15h in France), and they usually last for three or even four hours. You send out the invitations only a week or two in advance, or sometimes only a few days.

And then it was my birthday! I was NINE YEARS OLD!

'Dad, I want to invite Baptiste, Thomas, Frédéric, Mathias, Tristan, and of course Elliott to my party. Do you think that is too many kids?' It was really nice to think that I had a few friends that I could invite.

And it was *great* to have lots of my new friends over. We went to an enormous bouncy castle place and got really hot, and later we watched Mr Bean DVDs at home. Thomas and Baptiste laughed so much I thought they were going to make a bit of a mess on the carpet. Mr Bean is so great because there is no talking and no 'other language' to try and understand, and so it is really funny for kids everywhere, I reckon. It is just Mr Bean being crazy!

Back at school I found that it was a bit more interesting; probably because I was getting to know the routines and stuff. I was quiet though and just listened to the other boys' conversations. The school work still didn't make much sense at all, but at least I could recognise the numbers.

One weekend, Dad, Olivia and I went skiing in the Pyrénées mountains (pronounced *pi-ren-knees*) which are down near Spain. We went with Henri and Julie, Sophie and Tobi (so that they could help us work out what to do, and because they are nice). Mum and Dad said it was always a bit easier to take a French-speaking friend along with us the first time we did something or went somewhere new. After that we could work it out, mostly.

Skiing was awesome! Well, to start with, I *disliked it intensely* because I kept falling over.

But after one or two sessions of snow-ploughing with Dad I was zooming down the beginner's slope. I am definitely going to do more of this when I am older, in fact I really want to go on a skiing holiday for a whole week some time.

Dad left the car lights on – all day – so there was a bit of action and drama trying to find people with jumper leads who could help us start the car again. Mum thought that part sounded like *heaps of fun*, but she would say that because she was safe and sound at home with Edward who had a tummy bug.

I should mention that Toulouse has great museums (even I like them) and that every first Sunday of the month the Toulouse *mairie* has this free-entry-all-day thing. One Sunday we went to this medical museum where they had a *real* skeleton and gruesome, old medical instruments and photos of people with hideous diseases.

I felt really sick and I had to go and sit on the steps outside. I don't want to go there again. Ever.

I still have bad dreams about it, especially about the poor man who had this disease called 'elephantiasis' and had strange enormous shapes growing on his body.

Chapter 21 Six months later

We had been in France for six months.

'Oh, without a doubt, your children will be speaking French fluently in six months' time,' people had boldly predicted to Mum and Dad before we left New Zealand.

People thought that by now we would be speaking French like we were French? Huh?! No chance!

Apparently, the previous year, there had been a Spanish-speaking family from Chile in our new French school. Those children had learnt to speak French after about *three months*.

'But that's completely different!' I protested. I had read about this in a book so I knew what I was talking about.

'Everyone knows that French and Spanish are really similar because they both come from Latin roots. English and French are way different! There are lots of words that look the same in English and French but they have different meanings, and also the way you say words in a sentence is in a different order.

Anyway, fluent in French, in three months? You've got to be dreaming!'

Then suddenly it was the last week before the end of the second term. I would like to report that everything had gone rather well this term. But actually I found I wasn't doing so good. Every day I was having that bad feeling in my stomach – like I was going to be sick.

Some days I was so upset in the morning that Mum said I could have a 'rest day'. I really needed those, but I also really needed to find a way out of what was becoming a nightmare. The only good thing at the time was that I had started to learn the bass guitar, but I found it really hard because it was too big for my hands. I liked the animateur from school who taught me though, Jules. He could speak English and he was really kind.

I felt like I had become a STUPID KID, but I knew I wasn't. Even the other kids at school (the mean ones anyway) used to tell me I was stupid. They used the French word *imbécile* (I knew this word already from New Zealand), and worse – I couldn't even answer back! I wanted to tell them that actually I was a really clever kid who had just been dumped into this school in this new country with this crazy language that didn't make any sense to me.

'You try doing that!' I wanted to shout at them. 'You see how it feels! You find out how hard it is to move countries. Especially when you are a boy who likes-to-know-what's-what!'

Mum was getting a bit worried about me and was trying to work out how to help me. I think she could see that I wasn't really learning anything much. The mornings that I was absolutely desperate to stay at home were getting more and more frequent. I wished like anything that I was safe and sound back in New Zealand.

So Mum talked to my teacher and organised a meeting with the Secteur Education Jeunesse office again. They thought it might help if I chatted with another lady, Madame Durand.

'Matthew, darling,' Mum said one day, really casually, like we were talking about the latest book I was reading. 'A lady is going to come and check on you at school. She's like a teacher who has chats with kids who are new to the town, to see how they are doing. Just so you know.'

Well, as far I as was concerned, I was doing fine. I was just in the wrong country…(grump, grump, moan).

So Madame Durand pulled me out of class one day and had a chat with me.

'*Bonjour Matthew*,' she said, in French.

I didn't say hello.

'*Assieds-toi.*' Sit down.

I slumped in my chair and looked at the floor.

'My name eez Madame Durand. I 'eard zat you 'ad just arrived in France. 'ow are you finding zings 'ere?'

I wouldn't look at her or talk to her and I certainly wasn't going to tell her that actually I was starting to hear a few more French words, but *nothing* that meant I could respond like a normal human being.

'Do you like UNO, Matthew?'

I grunted. Then she asked me a few more questions, but I decided not to answer her.

'What do you zeenk about zat, Matthew?'

'Matthew?'

'Matthew, can you 'ear me?'

And after a little while of being aware of her talking to me some more, she said, 'Well, eetz zee end of zee term, and now you've got zee 'olidays. 'ave a break; 'ave some fun. I'll come and zee you again in two weeks' time.'

'Salut Matthew. Bonnes vacances.'

Goodbye Matthew. Happy holidays.

I sloped out, back to my classroom.

Still sad.

Still feeling dumb.

Still hating it.

And nothing had changed.

I cried heaps again that night, even with Dad cuddling me to sleep.

Chapter 22 More holidays!

At last, *les vacances scolaires* (the school holidays) arrived again. What a relief. NO SCHOOL! For two weeks!

I chilled out, slept in, read books and played with our new friends Nicolas and Jeanne. I must tell you about them, but it means a bit of an explanation first.

When we were in New Zealand Mum organised for this nice girl Camilla to come and help her out (when Mum was driven-to-distraction-by-three-small-children, she said). Edward was only a baby then. Anyway, Camilla became our friend and she told us a bit about her life.

She told us, 'When I was growing up I lived on a boat, and sailed around the world with my family; my Mum and Dad and my two sisters. We didn't go to school; our Mum gave us school lessons on the boat instead. And the only time we lived on 'dry land' was for two years, and it was in France in a city called Toulouse.'

I thought that was *a bit too much of a coincidence*: the girl who comes to help Mum once lived in the city we were going to move to!

Anyway, her big sister, Jeanne, married this really cool guy called Nicolas (he's half French, half Japanese), and they were living just down the road from here us in France. Talk about more coincidences…

Jeanne telephoned us one day. We *never* got telephone calls so it was a real surprise when the phone rang. We all jumped.

'Hi, it's Jeanne here. I'm Camilla's big sister. My husband, Nicolas, and I are staying nearby in Vigoulet-Auzil for five months (pronounced *vee-go-lay oar-zil*). It would be great to meet you; I've heard so much about you and your children from Camilla.'

And so we met. We saw quite a lot of them, and Nicolas played with us heaps. He was really good at ball games. I didn't really realise it at the time, but he was speaking to us kids a lot in French.

I actually started to understand some of what he was saying. Not everything, that's for sure, but a bit more. *And* I started trying to say one or two words. Jeanne and Nicolas knew quite a bit about learning new languages because they could both speak French, English and Japanese. I thought they were pretty awesome.

'Do you know what? I said to Mum one day. 'I really like Nicolas because I can try and talk to him in French, and he doesn't laugh at me.'

We went on some day-trips out of town together – Jeanne and Nicolas and my family and Nicolas's Mum. It was really great to see some awesome things, like Montsegur (pronounced *mon-ser-gurh*), a mountain-top fortress in ruins, where we climbed right to the top to the castle fortress. It was a long way to the top and it was a very hot day.

Dad told me that once, a long time ago, there was a big siege (battle) at the castle, and unfortunately it didn't end very well for all the people who lived there. They didn't have any great-great-grandchildren, if you know what I mean.

We saw a village built on the edge of some cliffs hundreds of years ago called St Cirq Lapopie (pronounced *sahn sirk lah-po-pee*), we walked under carved-out cliff faces next to rivers, and we picnicked in the evening sunshine. Sometimes I thought the sun was never going to set because it stayed warm and sunny for hours into the evening. At home in New Zealand, it would get cold as soon as the sun went down. And that was in the *summer*!

We also saw an incredible place called Peche Merle (pronounced *pesh merhle*), where we went into caves where people from thousands of years ago drew pictures of animals and spears and stuff on the walls.

There were drawings of their hands, with smokey-charcoaley shadows traced around them.

You've probably seen pictures of these drawings in books or magazines or on TV. I had, but it was really amazing seeing them up close, and seeing The Real Thing!

We saw the skeletons of animals that had fallen into the cave, or wandered into it, and we even saw a footprint of a kid about my age in some dried mud from thousands of years ago! It was freaky, but really cool. And it was cold down there too.

'Do you know what?' said Jeanne to Mum one day. 'I've been thinking about Matthew, Olivia and Edward and the way they are learning French. You probably know this already, but kids do learn better when they are happy and relaxed. Have you thought about letting them watch French TV? There's some cartoons on that they could just sit and relax, watch and listen to. It really helped me when I was learning French.'

Mum and Dad completely caved in at the thought of us actually being *happy* while we were learning French, and decided to let us watch some French cartoons shows, *purely for educational purposes only*, they said.

This was rather excellent news for us kids! Thank you Jeanne! You're the best!

We got to watch all these great cartoons like Road Runner, Scooby Doo, Tom and Jerry, and The

Pink Panther, even though they were all in French. But I guess that was the point! And I thought it was funny that BEEP BEEP (Road Runner) was the same in *whatever* language!

Chapter 23 Back to Madame Durand and more UNO

'Tu as passé de bonnes vacances?' my friends asked me in the playground.

Did you have a good holiday?

I was surprised to find things a little bit easier back at school. It was better going back there and seeing kids I knew, and knowing a few more of the routines and systems, and not being the novelty-new-kid-from-New-Zealand.

I was still not doing much work in class though, even though Madame Rousseau, my teacher, was trying to use some tricks to fool me into learning French. But she also had a very busy time corralling the other kids in my class, so she generally had her hands full.

Then this strange thing happened.

Wouldn't you know it, but after the holidays, and before I could say 'museums-are-free-every-first-Sunday-of-the-month-in-Toulouse' Madame Durand and I were laughing and chatting together. She was really nice.

And I actually discovered that she was really good at UNO too.

'Bonjour Madame Durand!' I said to her cheerily.

'Bonjour Matthew. Tu vas bien?' she asked me.

'Oui, oui, ça va, merci.'

HOLD THE PHONE! (SHREK again).

I just spoke to her in French! What's going on? How on earth did I do that?

What I didn't know was that there had been other forces at work in this whole situation. Before meeting me, Madame Durand had had a wee talk with Mum and Dad and she had given them some hints on how to help a young fellow who was struggling to adjust to life in a new culture. She said I might need to hear some *KEY MESSAGES*.

And they went something like this:

Number ONE: Matthew. Listen. We are in France. Mum and Dad have chosen to be here, and we are here for at least two years. That's the fact. You can choose to make the best of this situation. Or, you can choose to fight it and be miserable. You have to *accept* that we are here.

Number TWO: You don't have the option of going back to New Zealand. That's not going to happen, so you have to figure out how to make it work here, and Mum and Dad are here to help you to do that.

Number THREE: Sometimes you have to work really hard at something before you see results. You are absolutely, certainly, without-a-doubt capable of learning French. You were a good student in New Zealand and you will be a good student here too.

Number FOUR: Be brave. Be courageous. Do your best, Matthew. That's all we ask of you. And actually, it's a Really Great Thing to learn a new language!

She also suggested that I visit French friends, and have French friends over to play, and that I should get involved in team/group activities in the community. By one of those spooky-alien-invasion-coincidence-things, Mum had enrolled me in judo *that very day*!

The other good thing was this. I had told Madame Durand that I wasn't very happy with where I was sitting in the class. Sometimes a mean kid or two took my pens or told me I was stupid. It was driving me crazy.

So Madame Durand suggested to my teacher that I should be sitting next to someone in my class who could help me to understand the instructions for the work I was given. She even spoke to my teacher about it! Boy was she kind.

So I moved next to my friend Frédéric! And he started helping me to understand what the teacher was saying and explaining it a bit more to me and showing me what to do. Yeehaa!

Chapter 24 And just to brighten things up a bit, one day I had to visit the dentist – jolly Dr Dubois

He's really nice. Mum says he's handsome even though he looks older than Dad. He lived in America for a while, ages ago, so he can speak some English. I had to go and see him because my top teeth were growing down unevenly.

Dr Dubois is kind of like Dr Hibbert on The Simpsons because he laughs all the time.

''ello Matthew, I'm Dr Dubois (ha ha ha!).'

'Take a seat in zees chair Matthew (chortle, chortle!).'

'So zen, let's 'ave a look at zese teeth. Oh yes, zey need to 'ave some work done to zem (chuckle, chuckle, smile) and zen zey will be *im-pec-cable*.'

He laughed some more.

Actually, all that laughing was good because it made me feel a bit more relaxed when he fixed my mouth open with a special frame and started squashing sticky stuff like play-dough into my mouth and telling me to breathe naturally. I had to open my mouth, like, *really* wide. And then he told me to bite down on the dough stuff to make an impression of my teeth.

'Just relax Matthew and breathe normally, but don't move, don't sneeze, don't wriggle, don't cough, don't try and speak, and definitely stay calm and don't panic…(ha ha ha!). Now BITE! 'ARD!'

He was making a mould so that he could then create a plate that would fit inside my mouth to correct my teeth. He even let me choose the colour of the plate and the box it goes in. I chose blue of course, because that's my favourite colour, but they got a bit 'muxed-ip' and gave me green. At least it wasn't pink.

So this one day, I went to the dentist as a normal boy, and then I came out with this strange thing in my mouth. I was speechless – really, honestly, truly! I was just starting to try and speak a teensy-weensy bit of French, and now I couldn't even speak English!

I just gulped, slobbered and dribbled.

Chapter 25 Can you believe it? Suddenly it was the end of the school year!

Life (apart from school) was feeling a bit more normal and not so new and sort of 'raw' all the time. You could almost say that we were all getting used to things in our family and with our little routines. Mum didn't seem quite so completely bewildered all the time, while Dad was enjoying being a (very busy) student and meeting other students from different parts of the world.

There were lots of community events in Ramonville St-Agne like the Fête de la Musique (a music festival), and family things like our birthday parties. Sometimes we went to this English-speaking church in Toulouse. I met a nice boy there, Tristan, whose parents were from England, and we had lots of fun together. (He came to my ninth birthday party.)

And by some sort of miracle (or more alien-super-power-intervention), Olivia, Edward and I had all *somehow* passed our levels at school and in

September, when school started again for the year, we would all be moving up to the next level. I don't know how we did it (because even some French kids didn't move up), but I was really pleased that we weren't being held back. Maybe it was out of kindness so that we could stay with our friends, rather than for our ability because I sure didn't feel like I could actually do very much yet…

Edward must have learned some French because one night Mum heard him talking, saying, *Je m'appelle Edward, pas Jean-Pierre!*' which means, 'My name is Edward, not Jean-Pierre!'

He was sleep-talking in French!

We went to Olivia's end of year ballet show (she was *un champignon* – a mushroom, even though her costume was of a toadstool).

I had my end of year judo party, Edward and Olivia had their gymnastics shows, and we had a great end of year party at school called *kermesse* (like a school fête) where all the families from school came and played games, ate and drank, and chatted for hours in the evening summer sun (it stayed light and warm until 10pm!).

Dad almost got into trouble though. He and Mum went on a little trip to a hill-top village called Puycelsi (pronounced *pwee-sell-see*). They hadn't really seen each other for a while because Dad had been so busy with his studies and Mum was too busy working out the labels at the supermarket.

He and Mum were enjoying a nice lunch at a restaurant when Dad heard some people speaking with a really familiar accent.

'Hi there!' he said cheerily.

'Yeah, hi,' they said back.

'Hi, I heard you talking. You must be from Australia! We are from New Zealand. We certainly haven't heard your accent for a while!'

They paused, looking a bit puzzled, and said, 'Ah, no, actually. We are not from Australia. We're from New Zealand too.'

Let me tell you this: if there's one thing to learn in life, never mistake a New Zealander for an Australian. Or a Canadian for an American, or someone from Belgium for a French person, or a German person for a Dutch person…

And worse, Dad couldn't believe that he couldn't even tell the difference between a New Zealand and an Australian accent!

Chapter 26 Home to New Zealand for a visit

'Goody! We're going on the planes again!' all of us kids shouted happily.

Boy, I was ready for a holiday, and couldn't wait to see my friends and family back in New Zealand. I was really pleased that there were no exploding water heaters on the plane this time too. (At least I really hoped not.)

We left France in the middle of summer – think, 36+ degrees Celsius, which is over 98 degrees Fahrenheit – and arrived to winter in New Zealand (although, actually, the first day was quite sunny).

It felt really strange stepping back onto the earth in New Zealand again, like stepping into an 'alternative universe' or a 'bizarro world' or something. It was all perfectly normal, but so strange too.

Everyone spoke with really funny accents that I had never heard before. Apparently it was just the normal everyday New Zealand accent, but I had never really noticed it.

Some friends who had lived overseas for ages told us this story. Once they were at the airport in Auckland, back after a long time in Europe, when they heard an announcement over the loud speaker:

'Wud Muster Smuth pleyse cum to tha chicken counta?' they heard.

'That's odd,' they said to each other.

'Why would there be a chicken counter at the airport. Do they transport chickens on the planes now? Where would they be sending the chickens? It seems an expensive way to move chickens around; perhaps they are elite, exclusively bred, incredibly important chickens?' It really seemed a strange thing to do, or say and they were very puzzled.

Finally it dawned on one of our friends who worked out what the announcement had *actually* said. It was, 'Would Mr Smith please come to the CHECK-IN COUNTER.' It wasn't anything to do with chickens at all.

Boy, oh boy, if my New Zealand friends speak like that there is absolutely no way that I am going to understand them! I thought.

After a few days of being in New Zealand though, I couldn't even *hear* the different accent. And I thought it was really funny that some people said we were speaking English with a *French* accent! Ha!

'No, I don't zenk zat you 'ave 'eard zee French people zpeek zee Eengleesh – for real!' I tried to explain to them, pretending to have a really strong French accent, but nobody could understand me.

We had a great holiday on Waiheke Island, near Auckland where we splashed on the beach and had fun with a lost parrot-bird-creature. It was really friendly and we took turns looking after it with our cousin Lily.

And we tried to get used to sleeping at night again. That was an adventure. It took about five or six days to feel back to our normal selves again with that nasty jetlag.

A bit of fishing with Dad and Edward helped me to feel a little better, because I caught a lot of fish and found that I am a really good fisherman.

We stayed two weeks with Granna and Grandpa in Morrinsville and I helped them by digging up the weeds in their garden (there were *a lot* of weeds).

We saw some old friends, we saw Poppa, we went swimming in natural hot spring water at Lake Rotoma, and in the thermal water at Te Aroha Baths.

I did baking with Granna and I played dot-to-dot with Grandpa. Then, after a long bus ride, we stayed one week with Nana in Wellington and one week with my best friend Clive and his family.

We explored Wellington all over again like we were tourists. We visited the fun national museum Te Papa, Oriental Parade, and a nice little beach and a long wharf in Eastbourne.

I saw HEAPS of my friends and even visited my old Montessori classroom in Wellington for a morning where I noticed it was *really quiet*. I felt like I had never left, but at the same time, I knew I had this whole other life in France, and that felt really strange. But I *loved* seeing my friends again and it made me feel great to be with them.

Olivia and Edward were pretty happy to be back too. Olivia got to see her friends too and they giggled and played a lot, while Edward had a sleepover with his best friend Alec. Alec gave him some dinosaur pyjamas, just like his own ones, and Edward thought they were really cool. They were both really into dinosaurs then.

At the end of the six week it was time to jump on the planes again and get a bit of sunshine back in France. And the funny thing is, we were all happy to go back.

'We are going back home to France,' I said to Dad. 'I'll get to see my French friends again!'

Part IV On flailing and floundering

Chapter 27 The start of year two in France, and it was hot, hot, hot again!

We arrived back to France to find that our kind neighbour, Marcel, had tossed his children's old paddling pool over the fence for us to use. Thank goodness, I reckon, because just walking to the letter box to check the mail made me drip with sweat.

'My cheel-dren, zey are too beeg now. Zey don't want to play in zee paddleeng pool. Zey only want to talk on zee telephone wiz zeir friends. I zeenk zat your cheel-dren would 'ave more fun weez eet now.'

It's about the size of a table-tennis table, with high sides that you spend forever blowing up and running out of puff because you can't find the air-bed pump anywhere in the garage. Now, I ask you, was that a nice cool, easy way to spend an afternoon? No, it was not!

We quickly found though that we weren't the only ones who liked the water. The wasps loved it too! I don't know why, but every time we went for a swim, they did as well. It kind of freaked Olivia out because she's quite scared of insects and bugs.

'Get them away from me! Get them A-WAY!' she screamed. Actually, she *seriously* did not like bugs.

Sometimes the water got so hot from being in the sunlight that it was like having a hot bath. But we didn't mind.

We splashed around anyway and made heaps of noise and even put ice cubes in the water to cool it down (it didn't work).

And now that we were back we started having some fun with Jeanne and Nicolas again. We went on another trip to the Pyrénées mountains. They knew of this waterfall at a place called Gouffre de Saoule (pronounced *goof-reh der sah-ool*) that you could actually climb up to, and even stand *under*, so we got our picnic lunch packed and our togs ready to go for a swim.

What they didn't tell us was that the water was SO COLD that it would practically stop you from breathing. And then Nicolas threw me in the water and I almost froze. (Nicolas wears t-shirts even in winter, so he must not feel the cold like I do!) After that we had to lizard ourselves on the rocks in the sun to warm up, and of course investigate all the rocks in the shallow water to try and find gold.

Funny that I mentioned lizards because when we got back to France I kind of realised that there were heaps of different animals and insects here.

Maybe my brain had some spare room to notice things like that now.

Here are some of them: squirrels, woodpeckers, moles (and mole holes in the lawn), *gendarmes* (like lady-birds but not), snakes (brown grass snakes – harmless and timid) and lots of lizards that climb the walls and whizz along in the grass really fast.

There are also bats that fly to the trees near our house in the evening (good for freaking Mum out), big black bugs like *wetas* (really scary insects from New Zealand that look more like monsters, says Olivia), spiders that carry their babies on their backs (can you hear Mum screaming?), big, big 'rats' that look like cats and that can swim in the canal, and frogs.

Our neighbour, Marcel, brought over a box for Mum one night.

'Open zee box, Madame, and zee what eez inside. Eet eez somezing for zee garden.'

He was always giving her bits and bobs for and from the garden so she was expecting some seeds or a little plant or something. Suddenly Mum gave a great big yelp. She was looking at a frog.

While Marcel laughed his head off, Mum calmed down and said, 'Ah, thank you very much, Marcel, but…why are you giving me a frog?'

'Ah, but zay are very good for zee garden, Madame. Zay eat zee insects on zee tomatoes. Oui, zay are very good. And when you are tired of 'im, you can eat 'im. Ha ha ha!'

So, we kept 'im in zee garden but we didn't eat 'im. I know that French people *do* eat frogs, but I think Marcel was joking about that. I *think*.

We discovered figs about now too. I remember that whenever we went anywhere Mum was always scanning the countryside for fig trees. She said she was plotting a 'mental fig tree map' so that she knew where all the wild fig trees were. Then she would be able to go and plunder them after dark.

'Matthew,' she said, with this radiant, rapturous look on her face. 'Fresh, sun-warmed figs straight from the tree are the closest thing to paradise I can think of.'

'Well, figs and also fresh raspberries from the raspberry bush, new season asparagus, artichoke leaves dipped in balsamic vinegar and olive oil, oh, and large, juicy, dark red cherries…'

She would go on and on.

Man, I don't know what the heck she's talking about sometimes.

And I don't even *like* figs.

Chapter 28 So, back to school again for the second year, la rentrée

'Salut Matthew!'

Hi Matthew!

The day before school started, our friends – Thomas, Hugo and Agathe, and their Mum, Margot – biked around to see us. It was a really nice, warm, sunny day. We decided to all bike to school because the class lists were up and we wanted to see whose class we were in.

And it was great news! I was really pleased that Thomas and I were going to be in the same class. Phew! Our teacher for CM1 was going to be Madame Bertrand. She had helped me once when I had fallen over and needed some cleaning up and plasters and stuff. I had skinned my knee and there was even some blood, which of course made it hurt more than ever. I thought she was the nicest lady I had ever met.

Then Thomas whispered to me, 'Let's go and see Baptiste!' So we did. (Baptiste, Thomas and I were all really good friends at school, along with Frédéric too of course. Maxime, the brother of Baptiste, was Edward's best friend.)

We raced around to his house – just around the corner – on our bikes. His Mum, Marie-Rose, really loves kids and suddenly she had 11 kids at her house! She smiled contentedly, she let us play outside with clay and paints and stuff, she gave us drinks and then some more drinks, a snack to eat, and she smiled some more, until Mum dragged us away. She looked a bit sad then.

And let me tell you – it was COMPLETELY COOL to be going to my French school again!

Do you know why? Well, it was the *most weird* thing really. When we were visiting New Zealand I completely forgot about France and I certainly did not speak any French, even though people wanted me to, even *begged* me to sometimes. And then when we got back to school in France I found that I could understand *some* of what the kids were saying! And even what the teacher was saying! Not absolutely, utterly completely, but a whole lot more.

Dad reckons it's because we had a nice holiday and a complete break from learning all the time. Apparently your brain needs time to 'cogitate' and 'assimilate' all the new stuff. (Cool words!) And it seemed to be happening. Even Mum and Dad found the same thing.

Dad studied every day at university in English so his French developed the slowest of us all, but he did get a surprise when after two hours at a party he said that he realised he had been speaking French the whole time!

As for Olivia and Edward; well they were almost speaking French like the French kids now. They were definitely way better than me anyway, and Olivia was always saying, '*Oui, Chef!*' instead of 'yes', like she was a working in a restaurant kitchen or something. One of her friends in her class said it to their teacher once by mistake and boy did she get into trouble.

Edward was okay too. Madame Titine and Marie-Blanche told Mum after school one day that Edward gave an impromptu (without anyone asking him to) talk to the whole class about his holiday in New Zealand, and about the flights, and his friends, and volcanoes, and stuff like that, *in French!*

We had all sent New Zealand postcards to our friends in France, and Edward's class had his postcard of volcanoes and mountains on the wall for everyone to look at.

And Edward learnt to count to ten in English all by himself. Actually, at almost six years old he probably should be able to do that, but what was so funny was that he learnt to count to ten with the perfect accent of a French person counting in English.

Imagine hearing this with a strong French accent: *Won, too, zree, for, five, zeex, zevan, ate, nine, tehn.* Cool, huh?!

He had also learnt to juggle *two* balls (not three, just two, and he was really proud of that), and he was always kicking a football around or riding his skateboard.

He had already really grown a lot since we arrived here and he didn't seem to be the baby anymore. We played together heaps more now, especially as he was really good on his bike.

Edward had said to Dad one day, 'I can ride my bike without trainer wheels now Dad! *Please* can I ride without them?' Dad smiled, and just to humour Edward he took the trainer wheels off his bike and set him off along a flat bit of the driveway. And suddenly Edward was riding his bike without those trainer wheels in about two and a half seconds! It was great being able to zoom down the driveway together.

One day Mum and I dug a vegetable garden. We grew lots of herbs and vegetables and fruit.

Edward grew his own strawberries in the garden too, and he was really proud of them. They were really sweet and juicy and sometimes he would share them with me.

He did get some of the order of his words 'muxed-ip' though, but it was because that was how you would say the sentence using the French word order:

'I want to sit on the knee of Dad!'

'Ooh, I like that flower of orange, Mum.'

'Olivia had a bleeding of nose at school today!'

Olivia was in CE2. She was seven years old now. She had new French glasses from Fabien-the-Optician in the village of Pouvourville (pronounced *poh-vorh-vil*) just down the road, and now she looked really French, Mum and Dad and Fabien-the-Optician said.

Her teacher, Monsieur Lefebvre, was new to the school, and he had even played rugby once in New Zealand on a tour.

He knew about the Westpac Stadium in Wellington with the bright yellow seats (where we saw the French rugby team play the All Blacks) and he could speak a bit of English.

Olivia was right into her ballet, her gymnastics, her swimming, her chess and sometimes, her piano. She kept asking Mum to ask her ballet teacher if she could do a solo ballet dance at the end of year show.

She didn't like to read books very much though. Not like me. (I think it hurt her eyes a bit.)

One weekend our friends Dafydd and Patricia invited us to a picnic lunch by the Ariège river (pronounced *ah-ree-ezghe*), with some of their friends.

We met some nice kids – Hervé and Clara – and they could speak English! That was so nice because we could relax and not think too hard about what to say. Phew!

Chapter 29 Life ticks along

I was happy-ish. I was calm-ish.

I was *kind of* enjoying stuff. Mum signed me up for tennis, judo and swimming on Wednesdays.

There was a new system at school that meant that I sometimes had this extra tutoring on a Wednesday morning called *aide personnalisée* (personal aid) with my really nice teacher.

Every Wednesday afternoon, after judo, I got to go to my friend Thomas's house. We would have afternoon tea together which was usually some juice, and a wedge of French bread with dark chocolate squares stuck inside. (Can you believe it? But that is a quite normal snack here and it is DELICIOUS.)

Then we would play on the Wii for a while until Thomas's Mum said that it was time to run around outside and get some fresh air for goodness' sake. (Man, she sounded just like my Mum.)

Thomas and I would often laugh so much that I thought I would die! He and his brother really knew how to have fun.

And it was really great. Thomas's family were really kind and only spoke to me in French and I suppose they were giving me French lessons without me even realising it. I sometimes had lunch with them too which was cool.

'Bon appétit, Matthew,' they would say.

Enjoy your meal, Matthew.

We always sat down together at the table for lunch and had three courses to eat. And sometimes four! They would get their selection of cheeses out of the fridge and see if I wanted to try some.

'Matthew, would you like some cheese now? We 'ave zee *camembert, brebis, rocamadour, roquefort, gruyère, cantal* or zee *comté?'*

I've tried a lot of different French cheese (*le fromage*) now, and my favourite is definitely *brebis* which is made from sheep's milk (or 'the milk of sheep' as Edward would say). Thomas' family introduced me to lots of different food which was good because I have a big appetite now that I am 10 ½ years old.

Sometimes they were a bit crazy and ate lunch back to front - like dessert first, then cheese, then the main course, and then the starter! We all loved that!

Not long after we got back to France, Mum sang in a choir in an old previously-almost-tumbled-down-church called St Corneille (pronounced *sahn kor-nay*) in the little hill-top village of Puycelsi. It was a concert to raise money to help restore the church (which costs heaps of money to do because everything is scarily old and you need to be really careful and clever to fix that ancient stuff).

The church was actually quite amazing to look at with lots of gold and blue swirly decorations on the ceiling, but it had been badly damaged in places from water coming in through gaps somewhere in the roof I guess, and it needed some urgent repairs. Some *more* repairs anyway, as they had already done parts of it.

Mum sang something called 'The Messiah' and we heard some of the practice. It was really loud. I couldn't really hear just Mum singing though because there were so many people there singing in that warbly old-fashioned kind of way.

That day, while Mum was in her choir, Dad took us to a castle in a place called Bruniquel (pronounced *broo-knee-kel*).

We had to climb up quite a high hill to get there. There was a massively steep drop to the river below, but great views of all the hills and the tiny little houses everywhere. There seemed to be a church steeple in every little village, and there were heaps of little villages!

One tumbled-down-mostly-in-ruins-room in the castle was for the knights to get changed in. Yes that's right! I was in the Knights' Changing Room, where they got dressed ready for battle and possible injury or death! Completely awesome!

It was also COMPLETELY FREAKY. These guys were getting dressed up for battle even before any human beings lived in New Zealand (*hundreds* of years ago!). I liked to imagine being one of those knights, but I didn't want to imagine any battles because there would probably be blood and it would be terrible to faint in the middle of a big fight. And then I would probably be taken prisoner or something, and left in a tower, chained up, afraid and all alone, just waiting to die, with only a few skinny, hungry, miserable rats for company.

Then one day Dad said, 'Hey, Matthew. Do you and Olivia want to come with me to the Netherlands? We're going to take a train up to Paris, and then all the way to Amsterdam. You might get to take a couple of days off school.'

Well, *that* sounded tempting! Dad got out a map and showed us where it was. It was a long way, but it wasn't as far away as New Zealand so I figured it would be a pretty easy trip.

So we went to Amsterdam for the wedding of one of Dad's friends. It was cool, and we saw some really interesting stuff there like an old sailing boat with cannons, Anne Frank's house with the secret passageway to their hiding place behind the moveable bookshelf, a couple of museums, and the Amsterdam zoo.

I really liked the coloured, sugary sprinkles on bread that you have for breakfast even though Mum thinks it should be banned. I thought the French language sounded really nice too after listening to the people speaking in the Dutch language. Remember I said that the Swedish people sounded like they were speaking with soup in their mouths?

Well!

The Dutch people sounded like they were choking on a hair that was stuck in their throats! (Well to me anyway.) I had never heard anything quite like it before and it was a bit of a surprise. Mum says there are lots of Dutch people in New Zealand but I guess they have all lost their Dutch accents and say 'chicken counta' now too, like the best New Zealanders.

And then not long after that, we all made this awesome trip to see the Atlantic Ocean near Bayonne and Biarritz (pronounced *bay-on*, and *bee-ah-ritz*) on the west coast of France.

We stayed for a couple of nights in this kind of holiday-park place with apartments everywhere, and we got to have a splash in the sea. Because we are from New Zealand we know a bit about the currents and rips and stuff that can carry you off into the ocean.

Dad took a look at the wild currents near where we were staying and decided that we couldn't go right into the water.

We forgot to bring our towels though so it was gross getting back into our clothes while we were still wet from the waves splashing onto the sand.

The next day we found a perfect beach in Biarritz and got to do some boogie-boarding and playing in the waves – just like on our holidays back home in New Zealand. Mum supervised our clothes and shoes and bags and snacks and stuff on the beach which was her speciality, she said. She doesn't like swimming.

By the way, I'm really good at boogie-boarding. I learnt to do it at Matarangi Beach at the Coromandel Peninsula in New Zealand. Once, we spent an afternoon in the water having a splash around and zooming onto the shore on the boogie-boards, and it was great fun.

The day after that we saw a photo in the paper of *the very same beach*, with 50 sharks swimming not far from the shore! They were only little though, but, man! A bit scary! Dad said they were bronze whaler sharks so they might not attack us but they would still bite us if we wanted to stick our hands in their mouths.

We didn't. Of course.

Chapter 30 Christmas in France with my friend Gerard

'Kia ora Matthew!'

Hello, in the Māori language.

And then I was so happy! Some visitors from New Zealand arrived to stay with us for Christmas. It was so awesome to see them because Gerard, the son, was one of my best friends at school in New Zealand.

I almost didn't recognize him. When we left New Zealand he had really long blonde hair. And now it was all practically shaved off! I was growing my hair massively and his had disappeared.

Mum didn't tell me when he was arriving so when he knocked on our door, I just about flipped over backwards when I saw him.

'Gerard! What are you doing here? You shouldn't be here until tomorrow! Yiiiipeeee!'

We had so much fun together!

We went to Carcassonne (it was *freezing* cold and really empty because it was the middle of winter), Cité de l'Espace again (because it is just really excellent fun there), and we showed Gerard and his

Dad around Toulouse city including the Christmas markets at Place Capitole, in the town centre.

We took them to a city park (Jardin Raymond VI at St Cyprien) where there was a pond covered in a great sheet of thick ice. We tried to carry some home but it kept breaking.

At the park we enjoyed a ride on a fantasy, bizarro-world, wooden French carousel, like a merry-go-round. We also visited my school (even though it was the holidays) just so that Gerard could see where I went to school now. It felt like I was showing them around *my home town* because I knew heaps of things about the city and heaps of places to go.

I taught him to play pétanque too, with the new pétanque set we got for Christmas!

And Gerard's Dad made us laugh because on Christmas Day, instead of dressing up, he stayed in his pyjamas all day. He must have felt right at home! Mum made Gerard get dressed into his clothes though.

Chapter 31 And then, one day, the duck fat splashes off the barbecue and hits the hot embers and makes quite a bit of a smokey mess

'Matthew, are you ever given any homework?' asked Mum. 'I thought you would be given work to do at home after school.'

'No Mum, I don't get homework,' I said as truthfully as I could.

'Oh, okay,' said Mum slowly, looking really puzzled. 'So, why is there this list of work to do in your diary for the rest of the week?'

'Oh, that,' I answered casually, 'that's just to show us what we will be working on for the rest of the week, but we don't actually have to *do* anything.'

'Are you absolutely sure Matthew?'

'Oh yes Mum, absolutely.' I shone with sincerity.

The fact is, in my mind, *I personally* didn't have any homework because there wasn't a chance that I could do it. I absolutely *was not capable* of doing it. So I ignored it as being completely irrelevant to me. It seemed to be the best thing to do.

In fact all the kids in the class had to write these lists down of work to do for the rest of the week, and then study the work before that days' class; kind of like homework in reverse.

The storm cloud broke one day when Mum was having a coffee with her friend Margot. Margot said something about when she helps Thomas and Hugo prepare their school work for the week, blah blah blah…

'What?!' said Mum, all alert and anxious. I could just imagine Mum's ears pricking up and her homework-detection radar extending. It was those supernatural, alien powers again, I'm sure of it.

Well, that was that! That tiny, little comment there was the end of my 'no-homework' phase. Mum asked Margot to show her what to do, which books to work from, etc, and from then on I had to sit down with Mum or Dad in the evening after school and work through all this stuff. In a way I was relieved, because they could see what I should be doing, but on the other hand I was freaking out more and more because I was starting to see How Much I Really Didn't Know.

And it was looking B A D.

So, we continued doing this homework for a few weeks. Olivia too! She hadn't told Mum and Dad about this either, so suddenly it was very busy after dinner. She didn't have as much work to prepare as me though.

Edward didn't have anything to do because he was still at preschool. Dad was able to help us with our maths homework, even though he couldn't really read the French instructions, but he did manage to work it out because he's really clever with numbers. Mum was good enough reading our French homework and trying to translate it, and she helped us a bit.

She also had to translate our *cahier de correspondance* which is a book of information that the teacher sends home with notices and important stuff pasted in it. Mum had to read it, make sense of it, respond to it, and sign it, and then send the book back to school the next day – for all three of us kids.

If she read it correctly it might mean she could come on school trips sometimes too, which was good. She came on a trip to the Toulouse Sewerage Treatment Plant which she said wasn't exactly her favourite. She preferred the Musée des Augustins more which had heaps of old statues and paintings and stuff in it, and it wasn't quite so smelly.

Chapter 32 Red Alert, Core Meltdown Imminent – la deuxième (the second)

And then it happened. I started to feel sick again.

'Mum, why do I feel like vomiting and crying, even though I don't think I've got a tummy bug?'

I was getting this horrible feeling in my stomach every morning before school, and every night at bedtime. Sometimes I would be sitting reading my book and I would just start crying. It wasn't even like I was thinking about Grandpa dying or anything like that. Actually most nights I was crying and crying and feeling really worried, and in the morning I was really hyper – like I was wanting to go to school even though I really didn't want to go to school. I felt really weird and 'muxed-ip'.

Then, one night I was *really* upset (more than ever before). I was crying heaps and stammering my words out.

'Mum,' I spluttered and gulped, 'I just can't do school anymore! I hate it. I feel so stupid. I am *not* making any progress, even though you said that I would be by now!'

I went on. 'I seem to be the dumbest kid in the class, and I still can't really speak to anyone or make much sense.'

I really, really cried just then, and I almost vomited. It was *really* hard to talk.

'And the means kids are always teasing me. It feels like they are bullying me and it's horrible. They really hate me. And they deliberately leave me out of their games.'

When I think back on it, I was feeling really desperate; like I didn't know which way to turn or what to say or do, or something. I had to go downstairs from my bedroom and have a hot chocolate to try and calm down. Mum and Dad let me watch a bit of TV with them too. Eventually I got to sleep, in Mum and Dad's bed.

That week Mum took me to her doctor. Mum had found this really nice lady doctor, Dr Fournier, who spoke a bit of English. She had two children too, including a son my age, and she really understood kids. Mum thought it might be good for me to talk to her. Actually it *was* good to talk to her and I talked all about the stuff I had spluttered out to Mum and Dad.

Dr Fournier was really, really kind. She said I could talk to her again anytime I liked. She told me stuff like:

143

'You don't need to be the best; just give it a go. Don't be too hard on yourself.'

'So what if the other kids laugh? I bet they've never moved to another country.'

'Have fun. Relax. Do what you can. And perhaps it could be an idea to have lunch with a friend at their house, or to come home for lunch with your Mum sometimes.'

And Mum did that.

She let me come home for lunch twice a week, and the other days I went to a friend's house. These friends were here in France having moved from Romania, a country in Eastern Europe, and their boy, Alexandru, was feeling a bit strange being here too because they hadn't been here long.

It was so nice to go to their house and have pizza and French fries and play on the computer, and not have to think about school for two hours. They looked after me really well.

Then the time came for my next appointment with Dr Fournier. I went along with Mum. But it was funny because I didn't really *need* to see the doctor again, because of something really great that had happened.

Actually, I didn't think it was great at the time; because I didn't know what to make of it.

Keep reading. It will make sense soon!

Chapter 33 Complete meltdown by Mum this time

Even though I was doing a bit better by having a break at lunchtime, generally at school I was still kind of flapping around on the wharf like a half-dead fish.

After one night of much wailing, sobbing and gnashing of teeth by me, Mum said exasperatedly (which means not very calmly at all), 'I don't know what else to do! I don't want to have this grief all the time, and I don't like what it is doing to you, Matthew. So that's it! *I'm HOMESCHOOLING you!*'

YAHOO! YIPPEE! AWESOME! I thought. Fireworks of joy exploded above my head. I jumped around the house.

'I don't have to face all that school work and the mean kids anymore! I'll just hang out with Mum and learn stuff with her. Who needs to learn another language anyway?!'

I was *deliriously* happy. In fact I felt like a cat who was licking some cream with a little sugar in it, who knew that every night there would be another bowl of cream waiting for him, and who was lucky enough to have a soft pillow nicely warmed in a shaft of golden sunlight to curl up on, where he could enjoy the deep, contented sleep of the untroubled and the well-fed. (I was thinking a bit about Garfield or that weirdo creature in the Dr Seuss book, *Solla Sollew*.)

That is to say – I FELT REALLY HAPPY!

And that night, for the first time in weeks and weeks, I got to sleep with a smile on my face, and not a sob to be heard.

Chapter 34 Darned Dad and his level-headedness

But wouldn't you know it?! Dad had OTHER IDEAS.

'Let's look at this calmly, my dearest,' said Dad soothingly to Mum as he sat her down and topped up her chamomile tea.

'If we can get to the bottom of the problem for Matthew at school, then wouldn't it be better for him to stay there, and to achieve a victory?'

Dad can be incredibly level-headed at times, and I think it drives Mum crazy when she wants to have a little rant.

After a good long while and some fortifying dark chocolate treats, and a few more slurps of tea for Mum and red wine from Corbières for Dad, they worked out what the real difficulties seemed to be:

Number ONE: I had started school at a higher level than Olivia and at a higher age. So, I was expected to work at a higher level. CM1 level at school was actually quite challenging, even for French kids.

Number TWO: But I couldn't do it, because I had missed out on absorbing the basics, like a French kid would do at home with French parents and in their early years at school. The school hadn't had the resources to help me enough with the missing bits as we had hoped.

Number THREE: And I hadn't had the special language integration programme that we were expecting us kids to have when we arrived in France.

And here's the solution they came up with. They decided that I definitely needed some extra help to fill in the blanks, to boost my confidence and to help me stand up tall again.

I needed…A PRIVATE TUTOR!

Part V On surviving and smiling

Chapter 35 Annabelle, Annabelle, wherefore art thou, Annabelle?

So Mum wrote an email, and sent it far and wide (well, around Toulouse anyway and maybe even via South America, Norway and Bulgaria).

It said:

'We need to find Matthew a tutor to help him catch up with his French language learning – grammar, vocabulary – all the things he missed out when he was busy learning English in New Zealand.

'Matthew is currently in CM1, and progressing well, but he is struggling with various aspects of the French language. We think that if he worked through the French language resources for previous years, it would help him fill in the gaps.

'If you know of an intelligent, capable student who is great at encouraging, motivating and teaching 10-year-old boys intuitively and flexibly, please let me know. We are probably going to be in France for at least another year, so it's worth putting this effort in to help Matthew find his confidence again.'

I didn't know about this. I didn't think it was a particularly good idea at all. I was expecting to stop school and hang out with Mum doing the stuff that she does. That seemed like a way more cool life to me. (We could go for bike rides, have hot chocolates at the café by the canal in Castanet Tolosan (pronounced *kas-tah-nay toh-loh-zah*), go shopping for Lego in the city, do our own history tours of the old buildings, do baking at home, like *mousse au chocolat, cannelé, charlotte aux fraises*, etc. That's all learning isn't it?!).

Then an email arrived. Suddenly my dream of cruisey learning in Mum's company all day was completely and brutally shattered. And I felt pretty shattered too.

'Bonjour Madame Meade, je m'appelle Annabelle, j'ai 27 ans. J'ai eu votre email que mentionnait que vous cherchiez des cours de soutien pour votre enfant. Je serais très intéressée de vous rencontrer…'

And in English:

'Hello, my name is Annabelle, I am 27 years old. I read your mail looking for a French tutor and I'm quite keen to meet you. I studied for two years at the Mirail University in Literature and English, so my English is not too bad. I taught French to children when I was 20 years old, and it was a great experience. Let me know if you're interested in meeting me, even for a simple meeting. I'm living

near Castanet-Tolosan and I've got a car. See you
soon I hope! Annabelle'

O H   N O!!

Chapter 36 Tutoring

I wasn't sure what to make of Annabelle to start with. When she speaks English, it's sort of with an American accent, even though she's never lived in America.

She's quite clever. She's a musician and she's made her own CD of music. She's also a student, works part-time and wants to be a sound engineer. And she seems to have a bunch of different beat-up Renault cars and drives a new (old) one each time we see her. When my friends Thomas and Hugo were younger she used to look after them after school and they really loved her, so I thought that was a good sign.

She's often late too. I thought about this a lot. One day I couldn't hold back.

'Annabelle, can I ask you – are French people always late, or is it just you?' She laughed, and said it was just her.

But the thing is though, she is just *completely cool*. She really knows how to teach a kid. She's really funny and makes learning make sense, and has me laughing my head off at what she says. She even laughs at my jokes, including when I hide from her EVERY TIME she comes around, even though Mum tells me not to.

I have to say that Annabelle can be quite mean sometimes too, and she tells me to get to work when I just want to have a snack or crack a joke or get another glass of delicious sparkling Perrier water that Mum only lets me have when I'm studying. I make her a coffee when she arrives, although sometimes I need to wait until she's finished her cigarette before she will drink her coffee. (Lots of French people smoke, I've noticed.)

'Annabelle is my BEST FRIEND!' says Olivia. Annabelle helps Olivia too, after she's finished helping me.

And Edward is always showing her his gormiti toys or some crazy, wonky Lego car he's made. Mum and Dad sometimes ask her to make phone calls for them, or to translate some very important letter from a French bureaucrat at some big organisation or other in France.

'Annabelle,' says Mum. 'You are *indispensable*!' (That's the French word for 'indispensible' which means something or someone you just can't do without.)

Actually, it didn't take me long to really start relying on her too. We all did.

So every week I saw her on a Tuesday after school and on a Saturday morning, and each time we would look at the work to do for the next two days at school. We did this right up until the end of the school year, so for about six months. Then in the school holidays I saw her every day for two hours. Holy macaroni!

First of all though, she talked to Mum and Dad about me and what I needed to know.

'I wanna know what you zeenk zat Matthew needs to learn.' She spoke in her special American-English-French way.

Then she looked at my books from school. Then she looked at the homework I was given to do. Then we borrowed one of the textbooks from my teacher, and Annabelle set to work.

She explained to me what we would do.

'Matthew, I'm gonna prepare zee worksheet for you. You're gonna do az much az you can and zen I'm gonna 'ave a look at eet. If zere eez anyzing you 'ave got wrong, we're gonna 'ave a look at eet togezer. *Ça va, Matthew?*'

She had a really good way of explaining the French stuff that I needed to know, but she still had to repeat some things over and over again, until I got it. She helped me most with my grammar and conjugating verbs (changing the verb endings to suit the situation and who was talking, for example).

And let me tell you something very, very important. Anyone who learns their French verbs should be awarded an enormous, shiny, gold medal in a massive ceremony like the opening of the Olympic games or something, because learning your verbs is a DOG. In fact it's a really mean dog. A big-black-hairy-jump-up-and-bark-and-slobber-in-your-face kind of dog. You have to read these verbs, write them, recite them, use them, and then do it again, zillions of times, until you know them upside down and round the bend. Even French people find them difficult, so they tell me.

But then, French people do seem to like dogs.

Sometimes at night I would fall asleep with the different (big-bad-dog) verb endings going through my mind. Man, it was *so* annoying. So to crowd out the dog I started listening to 'Mozart at Midnight' on Mum's ipod, so that I could fall asleep and make those darned old barking verbs go away.

But wait! The good news was that working with Annabelle, well – *it really helped.*

(I told you it was good news!)

I reckon that Annabelle was like the MISSING LINK in my learning, and I was finally starting to make some progress as we kept working together, even though it was only little things to start with.

I kind of started *getting* more and more of what the teacher was saying in the classroom. It didn't seem to be this fuzzy, dreary, blurry, rainy, miserable mess all the time. I could see that through the fog there might be a teeny-tiny speck of light glowing.

Maybe THAT was the light-at-the-end-of-the-tunnel that Dad had sometimes talked to me about! I was starting to feel a little bit happier again, like it might just be possible that I could do all this stuff after all.

Imagine! I might have to stop complaining.

And…I wasn't crying all the time!!

Chapter 37 And then I found out that I am kind of French! How cool is that?!

'Dearest,' said Mum to Dad one afternoon. She was reading a book on the history of France.

'Tell me again, wasn't it your relatives, the French Huguenot people (pronounced *ooh-geh-know*), who were driven out of France by the revocation of the Edict of Nantes in 1685, in a brutal and bloodthirsty eviction?'

I stopped reading my Horrible Science book called *Chemical Chaos*. This sounded quite interesting too.

Apparently, way, way back many centuries ago in France, there were some people called the Huguenots. They were a large group of people who lived near Toulouse and lots of other places in France too. They were a bit different at the time because they weren't following the Catholic religion like most other people in France. They called themselves Protestants (which sounds like 'protestors' to me). The Edict of Nantes was like this law that said they could be Protestants, others could be Catholics and that that was okay.

Anyway, some French King called Louis XIV decided that he wasn't going to put up with their different ideas anymore.

'I 'ereby decree, zat zee old Edict of Nantes eez null and void; zat all zee people of France will now be of zee Cat'olic religion. Anyone 'oo does not like zis, should leave zee country, toot-suite.'

But 'e didn't give them much of a chance to leave zee country.

There were lots of battles against them, and lots of murders and butchering and slaughtering and raids and attacks.

Yargh! Blood! Death! Gory stuff! Heaps and heaps of people were killed. I guess it must have been pretty nasty.

But some of the Huguenots escaped and my Dad's ancestors (old family members from way back) were some of them. They ended up in England and then sometime/somehow they moved on to the country of Ireland; in fact lots of the Huguenot people ended up living all over the world!

And then amazingly, Dad's great-grandmother, who descended from the Huguenot people in Ireland, eventually ended up in New Zealand.

Once we went to a city called Montauban (pronounced *mon-toe-bah*), north of Toulouse, and saw the St Jacques church there where the King's soldiers once fired cannons at the Huguenot people sheltering from danger inside. The King had had a 'cunning plan' that came to him from a dream of a local visionary (some say a witch) that if he fired 400 cannons at the church all at the same time, the city of Montauban would fall and the King's soldiers would rule there.

You can still see the holes in the church walls where these enormous cannon balls hit. Awesome! (But kind of horrible too, don't you think?)

Maybe the King mis-counted though, and only fired 399 cannon balls, because the city didn't actually fall to the King's soldiers like the visionary-witch had predicted. She must have been having a bad day.

And then I had this bizarre thought.

'Hey Dad!' I said, all of a sudden. 'Maybe my great-great-great-great-great – *whatever* – grandparents were in that church! And then escaped!'

It was really weird to be there in the same place, and to know that someone I was related to *could have been there*, hundreds of years ago.

We might have even walked down the same streets! I wonder what they would think of me, if they could see me now. (They would probably tell me to get a haircut. I decided to grow it long because I didn't want Mum cutting my hair anymore – she kept cutting it too short.)

But what I really wanted to know was whether there was a huge old family castle somewhere in France with our name on it! Perhaps we could go and live there, and maybe we could dig up some buried treasure.

And, I wouldn't mind having a few servants!

Chapter 38 *Vive la révolution!*

In the meantime, big changes were afoot. There was a lot of muttering and murmuring at school. Thomas, Baptiste, Frédéric and I, plus another couple of friends, Mathias and Alexis, decided that we were going to stage a revolution.

We were so sick and tired of a group of mean kids telling us what to do, and taking over our games.

There were only three of them but they used to interrupt our games, push us out of the way, and tell us that they were changing the rules of the game – even if it was a game that we had made up! It was getting OUT OF CONTROL! And then other times they would make me deliberately lose a game by tripping me up or they sometimes ignored me and wouldn't even let me play.

It was outrageous!

I even had to go and talk to my teacher, Madame Bertrand, about it because they really started teasing me and laughing at me. She talked to the mean boys.

I was really surprised when they came and said sorry to me, and asked if I would play with them.

Wow – a big change (but I wonder how long this will last, I thought suspiciously).

And sure enough, it didn't last long at all. This whole pushing-me-out-of-games, me-getting-sad, me-talking-to-my-teacher, my-teacher-talking-to-them, them-apologising-to-me thing happened three or four more times. And they started doing it to my best friends, Thomas, Baptiste, Frédéric, and to other kids too.

I was getting ready to leave that school again. I just wanted to run away to where nice people were.

But wouldn't you know it but good old Dad had other ideas. (Again!)

'Now listen to me Matthew. Sometimes the best thing to do is to stand up to the bullies, to say no, and to tell them they have to play by your rules.'

How on earth was I going to do that?

'Matthew, did you know, that wherever you go in life, there will often be mean people: there'll be lots of nice people too, but sometimes life is about learning to deal with the bullies.'

What I didn't know was that our Mums (the nice boys' Mums, that is) had been chatting, and realised together that these mean kids were causing a bit of a problem.

'SOMETHING MUST BE DONE' the Mums all agreed. 'Boys,' they said to us. 'You can either let them continue to ruin your games, or you could go on strike and decide not to play with them.'

And then Dad talked to me about the French Revolution of 1789, and how the peasants (the poor people) in France got so sick of not having enough money, food, clothes, houses, anything really, that they stood up to the massively wealthy King Louis XVI and his wife Marie-Antoinette, and got things changed (after quite a bit of butchering and bloodshed.)

'Stop! Don't talk about blood again, Dad!!'

But we had had ENOUGH. We thought this idea of a revolution might just work but we would probably avoid the butchering and bloodshed as the teachers were quite fussy about keeping the classrooms clean, and I would probably pass out or vomit or something, and get really embarrassed.

So, Thomas, Baptiste, Frédéric, Mathias, Alexis and I hatched a sneaky plan.

We decided that if a mean boy wanted to play with us, we would say NO.

If a mean boy promised to play nicely with us and we said yes, and then he got mean, we would tell him to GO AWAY. We promised that we would all BACK EACH OTHER UP. All of the time.

It was kind of fun, but kind of scary too. I think we all realised that it was an important thing to do, otherwise we would be stuck with these guys bothering us every day, forever. But this way, *we* got to set the rules, and it helped that we all agreed what the rules were, and a big relief that I didn't have to

165

face these mean guys all by myself. We kept reminding ourselves of the rules, and we practiced saying these things to each other:

'Remember everyone, we get to decide who plays with us. We get to make the rules for our games. We will back each other up. We will say GO AWAY to someone if they start being mean in our game.'

But I was a bit worried that the mean kids would start picking on me again. I was still finding it hard to speak in French, especially if I had lots of attention directed to me, or if I was in a bit of a stressful situation, and they often laughed at me when I tried to speak French too. I stayed pretty quiet at school, except with my close friends.

Time passed. Three weeks' after that, Dad asked me how things were going at school with the mean kids.

'Oh, them. Yeah, it's much better now. We just kept saying NO to them interfering in our games, and in the end they got sick of it. So now we play by our rules. Sometimes we let them play, sometimes we don't. They can only play with us if they follow what we want to do. If they want to change the rules, they have to talk to us about it first.

'They are still a bit mean, but it was much better after we stood up to them and helped each other to do it. In fact, I might even invite one of them to my birthday party next year. He's not so horrible after all.'

Chapter 39 Holidays in the Pyrénées mountains

'Matthew, I've got some great news for you! Thomas's family have suggested that we go on holiday with them to the mountains for a week. What do you think of that?' Mum told me very excitedly one day.

We were so lucky!

So for one week, we joined our French friends, Thomas, Hugo and their little sister Agathe, and their parents Margot and Vincent, for a holiday in the Pyrénées mountains, in a place called Angoustrine (pronounced *ahn-goo-strean*). It's near the border of France and Spain which is to the south of France. We wouldn't be lazing around reading books and eating *chocolatine*, though. Oh no! We were going HIKING! (In French it's called *randonnée*.)

'I don't actually like walking very much, Mum,' I confessed to Mum one day. 'But because Thomas and Hugo will be there, it will be great! But please could you ask Agathe not to hug me all the time?'

We rented a *gîte* (a holiday house) right next door to our friends. I got to stay with them at their place (yippee!), because they had a big gîte and ours was really little and didn't really have enough beds. Actually, Olivia and I took turns staying with them because she got jealous and wanted sleepovers too.

Edward stayed with Mum and Dad. He wanted to have sleepovers as well, but they explained to him that if he woke in the night with a bad dream they wouldn't be able to give him a cuddle if he was all the way next door.

He thought for a while. 'No, I'll definitely stay with you, Mum and Dad,' he said firmly. 'If I don't have my cuddle after my bad dream, I'll have to start screaming.'

Margot had this great book of family walks in the area.

Each day we would pack our back packs with all sorts of things.

Water bottle – *check*.

Warm clothes and a raincoat – *check and check*.

Plenty of snacks, a delicious lunch, and a secret stash of sweets – *check, check and check again*.

We were set. Some days we were next to lakes and scrambling over rocks, other days we were climbing hills across farmland, and another day we disappeared into a forest or two. The best day was when we went up into the snow in the mountains! It was really fantastic. Us kids were always racing ahead in front, with one of the grown-ups. Only Agathe had to be carried sometimes but that's because she was little.

And at the end of the day we would light the barbecue and share some food together for a long and loud evening meal, and then play some pétanque on the driveway. Thomas had this crazy technique. He always wanted to be the last player of the group because then he could basically try to smash all the other balls out of the way. Sometimes it even worked, and he won! Sometimes it didn't though, and Mum won.

One day we visited the country of Spain; just across the border from a small town called Bourg-Madame (pronounced *borhg-mah-dahm*). Well, we walked about 100 metres into Spain anyway, so that Mum and Dad could buy some essential things like chewing gum and soft toys for us.

We had fun when we had one foot in France and the other in Spain – we were straddling the border!

'Hey Dad, look at me! I'm half in France and half in Spain! I'm completely split in two! Oh no! Where am I?! I'm *so confused*!'

It was heaps of fun jumping between the two countries with Olivia, Edward, Thomas and Hugo. Agathe was often with Mum, holding her hand. They really like each other, probably because Agathe's birthday is the day before Mum's.

There were lots of police on the border too, checking the papers of people going in and out of Spain. We thought that maybe it was because there were some reports of refugees leaving North Africa after some uprising.

The police even had guns. That freaked me out.

I felt like Tintin crossing the border to some new country, afraid for his life; afraid that the gangsters in the big, old car with guns out the window firing at him would catch up with him.

'Mum, have we got our papers on us?' I asked quietly and anxiously (whatever 'papers' were; I just thought it was the kind of thing Tintin would always have on him).

But we didn't need them. We must have looked okay because the police didn't bother us. I guess we didn't look like we were refugees leaving North Africa.

I got a bit nervous about that though and thought about it a lot. That night I had a dream about car chases, and Thomson and Thompson (in French, *Dupont et Dupond*) wearing their bowler hats and swinging their umbrellas, and bizarrely, about carrying heaps of heavy bottles of rum for Captain Haddock in my backpack over rocky mountain passes, trying to catch up with Thomas, Hugo, Tintin and Snowy who were walking way too fast…

Chapter 40 I just got my evaluation for my second year at school in France!

Guess what? I'm doing better than some of the French kids!

There's a grading system of 1, 2, 3 and 4. Number 1 means that you have 'acquired' or achieved the skill, while 4 means that you absolutely 'have not acquired it'. I didn't get any 4s. I didn't get any 3s.

I got mostly 1s and a few 2s!

And here's what my teacher wrote: it's in French, but don't worry, I'll translate it for you:

'Année scolaire très satisfaisante. Matthew a réalisé de gros progrés en français, à l'écrit comme à l'oral. Admis en 3eme année de cycle 3 avec toutes mes félicitations.'

And in English:

'This school year has been very satisfactory. Matthew has made great progress in his French. He writes as well as he speaks now. He has passed the third year of cycle 3 with all of my congratulations.'

Now that was just a bit earth-shatteringly astounding to me, don't you think?! If I didn't know it for myself, I would honestly think she was talking about another boy called Matthew Meade (who is *really good* at doing tricks on his scooter).

Chapter 41 And now, I present to you, the country of…New Zealand!

So, to recapitulate (that means to repeat).

My hands were sweating, my heart was racing. I could feel all these twisting, somersaulting bugs in my stomach, and they were really busy. I was in major panic mode because I was about to do something a bit uncomfortable. I was in front of 24 pairs of eyes, all watching me, all waiting for me to speak.

What if no words come out of my mouth? I asked myself.

What if I get completely muddled?

What if they laugh at my mistakes?

What if…?

I dithered, dallied and delayed.

I knew all of these people, but it didn't help. I laughed to myself for a moment, trying to distract my crazy nerves.

But now, it was now all up to me and I knew I had to begin. I couldn't delay it any longer. I took an enormous breath of air, gulped, swallowed and spluttered a bit, looked to Mum and Dad for support, and then began.

'Bonjour ma classe de l'école St Exupéry. J'habite en France depuis septembre 2009, mais je suis né dans un autre pays. Aujourd'hui, je vais presenter à tous, mon pays la Nouvelle-Zélande.'

And in English:

'Hello to my class at St Exupéry school. I have lived in France since September 2009, but I was born in another country. Today, I am going to present to you all my country of New Zealand.'

Dad and me had made up this cool presentation all about New Zealand on the computer. It was a like a slide show, and it was enlarged by a projector into this really big size on the wall of the library at school. It had heaps of interesting stuff about New Zealand, and masses of cool photos.

For the next 40 minutes I stood up in front of my class and presented all sorts of important, interesting and incredible facts, details, snippets, jokes, stories and so on, about my home country, about my life and about things that happen there.

But the awesome thing was, I was presenting it to my class completely, entirely, totally *in French!*

I explained stuff, answered questions, taught some words in *te reo Māori* (the Māori language), and the class asked lots of questions too.

We taught them some Māori words like:

Kia ora which means *Hello* in English and *Bonjour* in French,

Haere ra which means *Goodbye* in English and *Au revoir* in French, and

Aotearoa which means 'the land of the long, white cloud' and is the Māori name for *New Zealand* which is *Nouvelle-Zélande* in French.

They all did quite well, except for two things. In French there's a different sounding 'r', like you are hoicking something gross from the back of your throat (at least that's how you start doing it when you are learning but after a while it doesn't sound so disgusting).

The Māori way of saying 'r' is quite different – like it's an 'r' and 'l' mixed together. My class didn't understand the Māori 'r' so they used the French 'r' which made *Aotearoa* and *Haere ra* sound really funny to me, but actually they did pretty well. I didn't laugh at them because I knew that it was hard trying to speak a new language.

We showed the class how New Zealand and France have been kind of connected through the years, with the World Wars and stuff, and how New Zealand remembers all the soldiers who died overseas by wearing a red poppy on 25 April each year – ANZAC Day (which stands for the Australia and New Zealand Army Corps).

The symbol of the poppies comes from France, where fields and fields of them grow wild. You just about stop breathing when you see fields of red all waving in the breeze here in France, all of them remembering so many soldiers who died. It's awesome to see.

My Mum's grandfathers (Percy and Fred) both fought as soldiers in France in World War I, and my Dad's grandmother had brothers who fought in the wars too (Henry and Jack).

One of them even had his leg blown off in an explosion. Man, that would have been so horrible for him (and it makes me want to pass out just thinking about it), because good surgery and hospitals were really rare in the battlefields; they were pretty basic and there were no antibiotics to stop infections in the wounds.

I found out too that there's a little town up in the north of France, called Le Quesnoy (pronounced *ler ken-wah*) that has all these memorials to New Zealand.

I know! How bizarre is that?

But it seems that a week before the end of World War I (1914-1918) some New Zealand soldiers used ladders to climb over the walls of the village, and they rescued the village from the enemy (the Germans) who had been in control there for ages. So the villagers all have these special places around their town to remember New Zealand by. There's even some streets named after New Zealand places.

And in Cambridge, New Zealand, there is a very special memorial stained-glass window at St Matthew's Anglican Church of the New Zealand soldiers climbing over the walls of Le Quesnoy using their ladders. We've visited it! Cambridge, New Zealand and Le Quesnoy, France are twinned towns now, and they remember each other on Armistice Day, 11 November, each year because that was when the end of the First World War was declared. And there's a little 'French garden' at the church too.

I've been to Cambridge, but I *really* want to go to Le Quesnoy sometime now too!

Anyway, BACK TO MY STORY, even though I was nervous, I managed to speak to my class for ages.

Sometimes I forgot what to say but it was okay. Dad just said it in English and I translated it into French. Sometimes I got a bit muddled, but it didn't matter. I just said it again. Sometimes the kids laughed at me, but that was fine too – especially if I had made a joke in French!

But the best part was when Dad did the *haka*. He wanted to demonstrate this traditional Māori dance that heaps of the kids had seen on TV at rugby matches. (It was traditionally performed as a challenge by Māori warriors before a battle.) I warned them that it would be a bit scary and really noisy. But they loved it! Dad got a big clap after that.

Then we showed them a whole lot of little bits and bobs from New Zealand that Mum had laid out on a table for everyone to see. Things like an All Blacks cap, a Rugby World Cup 2011 scarf, a polished paua shell (a peacock-feather-coloured shell, also known as 'abalone'), some books about New Zealand because it's got really beautiful scenery.

There were some greenstone pendants (a precious stone of different shades of green used for weapons and decorations), bone carving necklaces, some toy kiwi (a flightless native New Zealand bird and our national symbol) that Aunty Helen had made, and a tui that sang the real tui song (another native New Zealand bird with a very nice little song).

Mum also used up the last ounce of our Vegemite (a breakfast spread for toast) to give the kids a little taste of a tiny Vegemite sandwich each. I handed them out and warned them that it was not sweet like chocolate, or Nutella which is a hazelnut spread. Surprisingly most of the kids ate it – I didn't think they would. I did a survey afterwards and 21 out of 24 kids in the class liked it!

It's really hard to find Vegemite to buy in France. I think you should be able to get it everywhere because we have to fill up our suitcases with it when we are in New Zealand to bring it back to France, and it's really heavy.

'Monsieur Meade,' said my kind teacher Madame Bertrand to Dad. 'I would very much

179

appreciate eef you could teach zee children to do zee 'aka. Perhaps we could move to zee outside to do eet?'

And so we did.

And here on the other side of the world, in a French playground, my French class was learning the haka in Māori. I thought that was incredible! My class really enjoyed it, and so did I. Then we took a photo to remember the day by.

Edward and Olivia's teachers both asked Mum and Dad to do a presentation on New Zealand to their classes too, so they were all very busy after that and Mum had to try and find some more Vegemite.

It was awesome for Edward and Olivia too.

That night as I was falling asleep I felt really proud of myself. I felt like I had climbed Mt Everest all by myself, crossed a shark-infested ocean in an inflatable boat without getting attacked, run through a field of thistles and stinging nettles and not got stung, fallen from a ginormous height out of a hot-air balloon and survived, etc. You know what I mean…

I JUST FELT GREAT!

Chapter 42 So, what had my family been doing?

Dad passed the second year of his PhD programme at university, and we saw him a lot more this year. I liked that. Next year he wants to be a rock star and play his electric guitar in a band! When he's not studying that is.

He smiles a lot to himself when his student colleagues tell him they think he is about 33 years old (he's actually 43), but he gets grumpy when some of his professors treat him more like a 20 year old.

He did some great bike rides along the Canal du Midi with each of us kids; all the way into town for a violet-flavoured-and-coloured ice cream from a special barge shop on the canal.

Mum helped some French people by proofreading some documents to make sure their English was perfect. She and Olivia also learnt to sing songs in Swedish, and they joined in with the choir for this year's Sankta Lucia festival, the Swedish Festival of Lights. I thought it was weird that Olivia and Mum could sing in Swedish but they couldn't *speak* Swedish!

Mum became brave enough to ask, *in French*, for fresh fish from the counter at the supermarket, so she thinks she's pretty clever now and can just about do anything. She does the shopping a bit quicker now because she can read the labels, and knows which supermarkets have New Zealand lamb (although I don't really mind because I have to say that French lamb is pretty good too).

Mum and Dad's French had definitely got quite a bit better, compared to when we first arrived in France that is. Mine was still better though, and so Mum used to get me to help translate stuff for her, or help her out when she got a bit stuck during conversations. And I thought that would *never* happen, remember?!

But one day Mum was speaking on the phone in French, as best she could, and Olivia was listening. After Mum ended the call she asked Olivia whether she understood her French.

Olivia said to her, 'Well Mum, you are getting a *bit* better at speaking French, and I could understand what you were saying on the phone, but your accent is…(shaking her head)…your accent is JUST TERRIBLE.' Poor Mum!

Olivia had her gymnastics show at the end of year, and her ballet show (she was a star, *une étoile*, this time), she had her swimming lessons and she started learning chess with her friends Brigitte, Lucie and Sofia.

She was always doing cartwheels or the splits or wriggling lots like she was dancing, and she drew these really cool pictures because she's so good at art. She won the drawing competition at the local supermarket for Mother's Day. She laughed a lot too, so I guess things were going pretty well for her. She got best-in-class one day for memorising and reciting a three-verse French poem about the seasons of the year. She sometimes set Mum homework to do too – like copying her cursive French handwriting. Then Olivia would look it over and give Mum a mark out of ten.

'Not *bad*, Mum…but there's room for improvement,' she would say.

Olivia now speaks with a perfect little French accent we are told. Once she went to a party and her friend's Mum thought that she was a genuine, born-right-here-in-France girl, because her accent was so good.

Edward did gymnastics too but freaked out at doing the show in front of everyone. He enjoyed kicking a ball around with his friends after school whenever he could, and he's going to start playing football next year which has a special uniform; he's pretty excited about that.

His favourite colour is BEIGE, and he loves his Superman pyjamas, even though they are not beige.

He had 17 kids to his 6th birthday party – lots of boys and girls (it was a riot), and he's got curly hair like his friend, Maxime. Some of his art, along with the rest of his class, was in an exhibition at the Musée des Abbattoirs in the city. It was all about colour and shape, and it was cool.

Edward also had this very strong local Toulousain accent which kind of made me laugh a bit. He must have picked it up from the teaching assistant for his class, Marie-Blanche, who had a good strong accent.

Instead of *le pain* (bread), he would say *le peng*. Any word with the '*ain*' at the end became '*eng*'. So a *Toulousain* accent became a *Toulouseng* accent.

But hey! He was speaking French!! I reckon someone from Paris would think he was a born-and-bred French person from Toulouse, rather than a New Zealander!

I think his accent will change a bit when he starts the little kids' class at my school in September though. He has 'graduated' from the preschool and he's pretty excited about finally being a big kid. One day he used the word '*undulate*' to describe the movement of waves coming in to the beach, so he must be learning something.

He said a big *merci* (thank you) and *au revoir* (goodbye) to Madame Titine and Marie-Blanche when the year finished. Madame Titine was very sad, because that was her very last day of her teaching life. She had been teaching for 38 whole years, and now she was going to retire and muck around in her garden and sing in choirs and stuff. Mum said she would have a coffee with Madame Titine next year when she starts missing all the kids (and now they give each other language lessons!).

I got a medal for my swimming, I finished my judo classes with a yellow belt with orange stripes and I played tennis in the sun, wind, rain and fog.

And wait for this – I even *danced* in a performance that our class made up! And we performed it about five times at different events in Ramonville St-Agne and in Toulouse. It was all about nature and wind and water and rain.

I finished the running races quite respectably this year; not first, and not second-to-last-in-front-of-the-boy-who-had-a-problem-with-his-leg, but nicely in the middle, THANK GOODNESS FOR THAT.

We did lots of training for that, and I wore my new tennis shoes, which helped a lot. And, of course, I knew what I was doing because I had done it before!

I went on a few school trips with my class. Dad came with us on one trip, to Cordes sur Ciel (pronounced *cord sir see-elle*). We had to climb and climb and climb up this steep hill to the old, mediaeval city at the top.

We had a guided tour (in French) which was cool. Dad fell asleep in the bus on the way home.

We finished this year with our school *kermesse* (end of year school fête) again. There were great games that you could do to earn tickets to buy water pistols and stuff. So we had these enormous water fights on the field and all got soaking wet. Even Dad joined in!

Like last year, the sun didn't go down until 10pm, which was about the time we got home.

On that same weekend, Dad had a few of his university friends around for a Sunday lunchtime barbecue. It was a really hot day – about 35 degrees Celsius (about 95 degrees Fahrenheit) – and some of Dad's friends even 'fell' into our paddling pool.

(All of them were young enough for Dad to be *their* Dad which Mum thought was funny until she realised that it meant that she was old enough to be their *mother*.)

Later we pushed Dad into the pool to cool down too.

'Hey, Dad! Do you have any phones or other electronic devices in your pockets?' I asked him casually and calmly before we pushed him into the water. (He should have said *yes*!)

And we stayed there for ages, all five of us.

Chapter 43 Two years later – what do I think of France?

The other day Mum said, 'I wish I had a time machine.'

I have to say that I kind of ignored her because this is another one of those things that she's always saying. She wishes she could travel back in time and see ancient civilizations, and meet people from her family from years ago, and wear weirdo, old-fashioned clothes and stuff.

She also wants to drain all the world's oceans to see what's under all that water and see where all the treasure is, *and* she wants to know all the secrets of the universe and if there's life somewhere else and whether she could visit other planets and talk to the aliens. But that's definitely another story.

Anyway, so Mum said, 'I wish I had a time machine. I wish I could put all of you kids in the time machine and take you back two years to when we arrived in France; when everything was strange and you couldn't speak French. Do you remember how much you hated it? Do you remember how difficult you found it, and how you used to cry all the time?'

Well, to be honest, I couldn't remember. I stopped checking the TV schedule to find out when Top Gear was next on.

'Well Mum,' I said, 'I do really, really miss New Zealand'.

'Oh my darling sweetheart boy,' said Mum, feeling *really* bad about dragging me away from my safety, my security, my life, my joys.

'What is it that you miss most about New Zealand? Is it your friends at school? Is it the beaches, your old house, the holidays we had, your dear, dear, old grandparents? Tell me Matthew, and I'll help you! I'll comfort you!'

'No Mum it's not that at all. What I really miss is all my toy cars and trucks. Can we get them out of storage when we go back to visit?'

And then I thought a bit more.

'Actually, Mum, I enjoyed France the minute we arrived. Learning French hasn't been difficult at all. I really love it here and I've got heaps of friends. No, honestly, it hasn't really been hard for me at all.'

Then this weird thing happened. Mum kind of slid off her chair, onto the floor, and sat there with a stunned-mullet look on her face. She asked Dad for a restorative glass of something really strong, and I don't think she meant milk with extra calcium.

Man, who's making a drama of things now, I thought. She can be *so* dramatic sometimes.

Chapter 44 Final thoughts

I like France.

And I really like my French friends.

I also like that I am from New Zealand and that I have a whole other life there when we go back for holidays.

I like that I can think and speak and write and play in two languages. I can watch movies in two languages and get the jokes! I even know swear words in two languages (not that I'm supposed to use them), and now that I'm a bit older I think that's all pretty cool. Sometimes Edward wants to watch movies in *another* language, like Portuguese, because he's decided that since he has learnt French, he can learn a third language too!

I'm not quite ready for that yet.

I do miss Grandpa, Granna, Nana and Poppa though. And all of my New Zealand friends.

I know Mum laughs (cries) when she thinks about all the changes we've had to make, but we're okay.

And Dad says that he is 'really, really happy to be giving his kids the opportunity to experience life in a different culture'.

'Life changes, Matthew darling,' Mum and Dad say when they are being all thoughtful, sitting outside in the evening stillness and sun, enjoying a drink.

'Nothing stays the same, and friendships come and go. It's a really good thing to completely enjoy and appreciate what you have around you, and the friends you have, *right now*, because this time of your life won't last forever.'

I can kind of understand what they mean, now that we have left my old friends in New Zealand. I can really see that life *does* change.

And I really didn't know if I would like it here, or that I would end up kind of looking like the French boys a bit more with that long, floppy fringe thing going on, and of course you know that my parents tease me about that (remember, those *cat* jokes).

In fact, I think I have *plus de courage* (more courage) now, and it's pretty cool to be here.

AND THAT IS THE END OF MY STORY!

P.S.

p.s. Actually, what I want to do next is a great big road trip through France, with my family, visiting all the places that have a bit of a connection with New Zealand, like the Somme battlefield, the village of Le Quesnoy, some tunnels that were dug by New Zealand soldiers, etc, etc. There is heaps to see and do, and that would be so cool!

p.p.s. Next year in France I will be going to collège, and I've heard it's really hard. What's *that* going to be like?! Oh man!

Appendices

Appendix 1 *A bit about school in France*

School starts at 9.00 am (at my school) but kids can be dropped off anytime from 7.45 am so that their parents can get to work. All the schools have different systems and sometimes they start earlier and finish earlier.

The animateurs are there before school, at lunchtime (during meal times and play times) and after school, and they help supervise and play games with us. Mum says she reckons it's a great system because the teachers get a break during the day and aren't responsible for looking after the kids all the time.

We work hard in our classrooms (with a little run around and quick snack break mid-morning) until lunchtime (midday).

The lunch break at my school is two hours long which seemed a lot to me to start with but quite normal now. Because I am one of the older kids I get to play for an hour and then at 1.00 pm I go with the other older kids to eat lunch. The little kids eat first and play later.

(I'll tell you more about the canteen soon).

After that we work from 2.00-5.00 pm and we have another little run-around-eat-something-quickly break in the middle of the afternoon too. When the bell goes at 5.00 pm we can go home. Or not! Some kids get picked up at around 5.00 pm, while some kids go into the after-school care programme with the animateurs anytime until 6.15 pm. They can play or work on their homework.

It's a pretty long day! But the totally cool thing is that we only go to school on Monday, Tuesday, Thursday and Friday. We don't have to go to school on Wednesday!!

That's one whole day off school each week!!

It may mean that we spend ages at school each day, but it also means that we do most of our *extra-curricula activities* on a Wednesday (although sometimes we do stuff after school as well). Some schools do have school on a Wednesday but it is usually only in the morning.

There are heaps of activities that we do on a Wednesday. Sometimes it can get a bit confusing though – tennis, swimming, judo, gymnastics, ballet (Olivia not me), chess…? It's just lucky that I'm in the car with Mum so that I can remind her where we are going.

I don't know what she would do without me.

And you should know too that at school there is no playground equipment like climbing frames or monkey bars or stuff like we were used to in New Zealand at school.

Instead the kids play marbles or bull-rush or football or basketball, or this game on a table tennis table where you knock a soccer ball over the net to try and get the other person out. It was strange without the playgrounds I was used to, but it's quite normal now. We just have fun in a different way.

My school is named after a famous French aviator-explorer and author, Antoine de St Exupéry. He wrote *Le Petit Prince* a famous French book. We've even got illustrations from the book painted on the outside of our school. And there's a quote from the book that everyone here seems to know, and they say it at the oddest times. It is, '*Dessine-moi un mouton!*' which means 'Draw me a sheep!'

Huh?!

All the kids here have those wheelie bags for school too, like they are going on a plane or something. I thought it was odd but it actually makes sense because the school books are so heavy, and there are so many of them that it's the best way to move them. My bag is super impressive because when you move it along, there are flashing lights in the wheels.

What kinds of stuff do we learn at school? Well we learn about French history (the Gauls, the Romans, the Kings and Queens, and the way people used to live), French language (spoken, written and

French literature and poetry), English, mathematics, geography (France, mostly at this stage), dancing (sometimes), and sports. A random quick look in my school diary one day showed that we were studying history – *des peuples barbares en Gaule* and *les grandes invasions*, (the barbarian people of Gaul, and the grand invasions) – cool!

When we have our English lessons we have a different teacher who is 'specially trained' in teaching English even though she is French. I have to say that my English is A WHOLE LOT BETTER than hers and sometimes she has asked me to give real live demonstrations on how to say something in English. Olivia and Edward do that too. I think all the kids in my school will end up with a New Zealand accent like us.

Do I need to mention that English is my best subject…?! Although now I'm pretty good at reading and memorising French text and poetry by heart, and then reciting it in front of the class!

And when do we have our holidays? I was used to the school year starting in February in New Zealand, and we kept going all through the year until December, apart from the term breaks of course. Then we had Christmas and the long school holidays in the summer sun and warmth (if we were lucky with the weather, that is).

Here in France school starts in September at the end of summer, after two months of gloriously warm and sunny holidays. The start of the school year is a really big deal *(la rentrée)* and all the shops have special sales and advertising for all the latest and coolest school gear and stuff.

The holidays have these great names. After the long summer holidays that here last about two months we also have regular breaks throughout the year. They are called: *Toussaint* (Autumn); *Noël* (Christmas); *Hiver* (Winter), and *Printemps* (Spring).

Appendix 2 And what about the school holidays?

And yes! Then there's the school holiday programmes! There are so many cool things you can do, as long as your Mum remembers to book you into them on time because there are lots of kids wanting to do them from Ramonville St-Agne and other villages nearby.

On one holiday programme me and Olivia learnt fencing – not New Zealand fencing where you go to the back of a farm and build a fence, but with a sword! It's called *escrime* in French. You get to stand in a really funny position and kind of shuffle backwards and forwards like a crab (well, crabs shuffle sideways so it is a *bit* different).

On another holiday Olivia did *escalade* which is indoor rock-climbing. She loved it and was really good at it even though Mum wouldn't pay 50 euros to buy her the right shoes when she was only doing it for one week for heaven's sake.

We don't go to holiday programmes all the time. Sometimes we just hang out at home and ride our bikes, scooters and rollerblades up and down the drive. We get really hungry so Mum is always making us stuff to eat or baking with us.

Remember I said there was no school on a Wednesdays? Well, Edward goes to a regular holiday programme on Wednesday mornings during the school term, and all day in the holidays. It's at the Centre de Loisirs (which kind of means leisure centre). The animateurs from school go there and do heaps of great activities with the kids. I went there a few times, and we did things like a disco, a trip to the movies, a bike ride along the canal, and a day trip to the ice-skating rink, plus heaps of other activities like sports, art, baking, etc. Cool!

The best programme me and Olivia did though was on this farm called Ferme de Cinquante, in Ramonville St-Agne. They keep lots of animals there and we got to learn about them and feed them and do different activities like baking bread.

But wait for this!

We saw a big pig bite another pig's tail off (it's true!). This big pig was trying to show the other two pigs that *she* was the dominant one.

Me, Mum, Olivia, Edward were there watching the pigs being fed when suddenly this pig (with the tail being bitten off) starting squealing like a hurt baby. It was awful.

Edward leapt about two metres through the air and into the arms of Mum because the pig was squealing so horribly. Olivia and I jumped too. There was blood everywhere and it made me feel sick. I'll *never* forget that!

But it was really great there.

Appendix 3 School lunches and the canteen

In France it seems to be very important that kids at school all sit down at a table and have a hot meal served to them at lunchtime. That's really different from the bring-your-own-lunch-to-school-every-day thing in New Zealand, that's for sure.

In New Zealand none of the schools have a school canteen like they do in France (maybe one or two do, but mostly they don't). So every morning (or the night before) you (or hopefully your Mum or Dad) make your lunch: a sandwich, yogurt, cheese, fruit, biscuits, or something like that.

In France, that kind of lunch is called a *pique-nique* (like the English word 'picnic') and here we sometimes have them as a special treat! So if we go on a school trip somewhere we usually bring our own *pique-nique* from home, which I have to say is a bit of a novelty for the kids in my class. Lots of the kids seem to have stacks of sweets (*les bon bons*) in their lunch bags too.

Each month a menu list is sent to all the schools in Ramonville St-Agne with the food that will be served each day. We check the menu list every morning when we get to school to see what we will be eating that day. Each meal begins with a starter *(entrée)*, then a main course *(plat principal)* and ends with dessert *(dessert!)*.

We have organic food *(biologique)* and some vegetarian meals too.

The meals are prepared at a central kitchen in Ramonville St-Agne and delivered to the schools. The little kids eat at the first service. They are seated at tables and served their meals by the canteen staff, who all wear white coats.

Olivia says she can tell what's going to be for lunch that day just by looking at the 'menu on the floor' (the food the little kids who eat before us have dropped).

Here are some examples of the different courses we have each day:

Entrée

Betteraves Rouges et Crème Fraîche (beetroot with a sour cream sauce),

Asperges Vinaigrette (white asparagus with a vinegar dressing),

Concombres au Yaourt et Ciboulette (cucumber in a yoghurt and chive dressing).

Plat principal

Tajïne d'Agneau aux Amandes, et Couscous (Moroccan lamb with almonds and couscous),

Lapin à la Provençale, et Courgettes aux Herbes (rabbit in the provençale style, with herbed courgettes),

Pavé de Saumon au Basilic, et Haricots Verts Sautés (salmon with basil and sautéed green beans).

Dessert

Fromage Blanc et Confiture (soft cheese – like yoghurt – with jam),

Flan Vanille et Fruit (vanilla flan served with fruit),

Mousse au Chocolat et Biscuit (chocolate mousse and a biscuit).

Oh, and, we always have French bread with our meal – of course! We use it like a knife – to push our food onto our forks, and to mop up the delicious juices and sauces. We don't have little side plates for our bread; it rests on the table by our big plate and we just tear a piece off when we want some and then rest it back on the table. That's quite normal here.

Edward wants bread like that at every meal at home now too, and even Dad thinks it's a pretty good idea.

Appendix 4 Some things about France that I have noticed

Cars

I like cars. There's lots of Renault cars, Peugeot cars and Citroën cars here in France, and you don't see so many of them in New Zealand.

They are usually little, and they are usually being driven so fast that they are a complete blur and a roar. Most cars in France have dents and scratches. Our car is *very* French.

It's unusual to see cars that aren't French here, although Mum just happens to drive a British Rover car that has the steering wheel on the *normal* side of the car (right hand side, like in New Zealand).

She gets lots of alarmed looks when drivers notice that there is NO DRIVER on the left hand side of our car, or me sitting in the front seat because I am definitely too short to be driving. Mum says they do a 'double-take'.

Some of the gypsies who beg for money at the traffic lights get a bit of a surprise too.

Once Mum and Aunty Angela (who was visiting us in France) saw a dog driving a car! Well, they thought they did. Actually the driver was sitting on the French side of the car to drive; it was the dog that was in the passenger seat. They laughed a lot about that.

Culture shock

I don't really know what that means. All I know is that things look different here. Nothing is written in English, or if it is, it is for *novelty advertising purposes only*, Dad says. So to start with you get used to seeing stuff that you don't understand at all.

In fact you get really good at just looking and listening, and being massively tired for about the first year.

French culture

Mum is always going on about how much she loves it.

As far as I can see, no one here is any more 'cultured' than in New Zealand. The kids eat with their mouths open and try to talk at the same time.

Sometimes I want to move tables at school in the canteen because I'm getting sprayed with food while my friends are talking. Gross.

There's too much rubbish everywhere too and my sister and Mum are quite worried about that.

Food and drink

The food here is quite good and you get to eat more duck and rabbit and turkey and lots of Toulouse sausages and *cassoulet* and *foie gras*.

Dad says that drinking alcohol here is not the big deal it is in New Zealand (or at least people drink in a different way - whatever that means). Maybe it means they drink alcohol here to wash the cassoulet down, rather than to get drunk.

Family

What I do see here is that families really seem to like being together and doing stuff as a large group with all their friends. People are generally quite respectful of older people too and seem to use the polite form of the French language. People in the shops are mostly really friendly and helpful too. And it's really important to bisou grownups (you know, that kiss on each cheek thing), especially when they come to visit you or when you go to their house.

History

I can see too that people have lived in France for ages and ages! Like hundreds and hundreds of years. That's really interesting to think about, and now we have to learn about it at school too. I know stuff about the kings of France now and the years they were in power.

There's mind-blowingly old places to visit too and amazing things to see like the old Roman arenas where people were killed by other people or very hungry animals. Yuck.

I read lots of Horrible History books too (in English) and I can kind of understand stuff better when they talk about France because I am here and can see it. That's cool.

Appendix 5 Some recipes that you might like to try

I can make some really yummy French food now. Mum likes cooking and baking and she lets me help her. I can make some of these by myself!

Salad with French Dressing

Get some salad greens from the garden or the supermarket, washed, spun and drained well. Then throw them all into a big bowl.

For the French dressing put ½ teaspoon whole grain mustard (or fine mustard) into a little cup, add 3 teaspoons of balsamic vinegar and then very, very slowly add about 6 teaspoons of olive oil while you beat the heck out of the mixture with a little spoon. This makes sure that the oil combines nicely with the vinegar and mustard.

Toss this dressing through the salad just before you put it on the table for everyone to eat.

Carrot Sticks with a Herby Dip

Peel a whole lot of nice carrots and top and tail them. Then slice them into little sticks.

Go to the garden and get some chives, parsley and thyme leaves and chop them all up.

Put some fromage blanc into a bowl and add some salt and a splash of olive oil and a squeeze of lemon juice.

Finally mix in the herbs and you've got your herby dip. It's nice.

French Toast

Use any old French bread like baguette or flute, or your normal bread.

Dip the bread in beaten eggs, a little brown sugar and cinnamon that you have mixed together really well.

Then gently fry the bread in a fry pan with some butter.

Easy! It's very *yum yum* with maple syrup.

Croque Monsieur

This is a toasted sandwich with cheese and ham, either in a toasted sandwich maker or in a fry pan with some butter. Fry it on both sides!

Fondant au Chocolat

250g butter, 250g dark chocolate, 250g sugar, 5 eggs, 1 tablespoon of flour. Melt the butter and chocolate together. Take off the heat and add the sugar and the five eggs and mix well, then add the flour. Pour into a cake tin and cook slowly at about

170-180 degrees Celsius for as long as it takes so that the cake isn't too wobbly in the middle.

Let it cool a bit before serving with cream or berries or ice cream or with everything! I can't eat too much of it because it is so rich, and that's even when I really try hard to. Once Mum made it and completely forgot to put any butter in, and it still worked and it was really delicious!

Cannelé (you might see them called *canelé, canelet* or *cannelet* too)

1 litre milk, 100g butter, 500g caster sugar, 4 egg yolks, a vanilla pod or 1 teaspoon vanilla essence, 150ml rum if you want to, 300g flour. You make the mixture one day and then let it sit in the fridge overnight. So, put the milk, and butter (and vanilla pod or vanilla essence) in a saucepan and slowly melt the butter. Take off the heat and add the egg yolks and mix well.

Then add the sifted flour, sugar and rum and mix well. Leave overnight, covered, in the fridge.

The next day, pour the mixture into special cannelé moulds which are either the big ones or the mini ones. Only fill them 2/3 full or they will overflow and burn on the element of the oven as we cleverly found out.

Or, you could put a baking tray under the cannelé tray.

Then bake in a hot oven, 200 degrees Celsius (400 degrees Fahrenheit) for about one hour, until they are kind of nicely caramelised around the outside.

Turn them upside-down onto a cooling tray and let them cool down before tucking into them and gobbling them up.

They are also called Bordeaux (pronounced *bor-doh*) sweet puddings.

Charlotte aux Fraises

Get lots of little sponge fingers (about 20-30) also called *boudoirs* or *lady fingers*, lots of fromage blanc, fresh or frozen berries, and some whipping cream. Put 2 tablespoons of sugar into about a cup of water in a bowl. Dip each little sponge finger into the water and quickly take it out and line the base and edge of a special charlotte aux fraises mould, or a bowl.

When you've lined them in a circle all around the mould or bowl, scoop in heaps of fromage blanc or plain yoghurt or cream, and lots of fresh or frozen berries. You could also add some grated chocolate or chocolate drops, or some grated lemon zest.

Then put a layer of dipped sponge fingers over the top of the goodies underneath and press it down hard with a plate, or with the lid to the special mould. Put it in the freezer to freeze.

When it is nicely frozen, unmould the mould, or tip the bowl upside-down onto a plate, and eat with cream or some more berries or a chocolate sauce. It *will be* delicious!!

One day our friends Thomas, Hugo, Agathe and their Mum, Margot, came to visit and Mum gave them some cannelé that she had made. Later, Hugo (who loves food and wants to be a chef when he's older) asked his Mum if they could make some too, but Margot said that she had never made them before and didn't know how to make them.

So they phoned Mum and asked, 'Pleeze could you come to our 'ouse and show us 'ow to make zee cannelé?'

So we all went around to their house and made cannelé. About one hour later, when they had cooled down, we (Margot, Thomas, Hugo, Agathe, Mum, Olivia, Edward and me) ate them all. They disappeared VERY QUICKLY.

They were so delicious, and actually I reckon that Mum and Margot's ones are nicer than the shop ones. There are *whole shops* here that only sell cannelé because they are so popular in Toulouse!

Margot, Thomas and Hugo's Mum makes the best Charlotte aux Fraises too. That's her recipe that I've written above.

Appendix 6 A few French words that I have learnt

This is a list of really useful words and phrases that I thought might help you a bit if you are ever thrown into a French school *against your will* without knowing a scrap of French. I really hope this helps.

Qu'est-ce que c'est que ça?	It's pronounced *kesker sek sa?* and means (in the short form) **What's that?** I think it's really funny that all those strange words and letters mean such a small question!
Bonjour	**Hello**. You should always say **Bonjour** to people (pronounced *bon-jurh*).
Salut, Salut	One means **Hi** and the other means **Bye**. They are both pronounced *sah-loo*. You would say it to your

friends.

'ello This is the French way of saying **Hello**. You hear it when people answer the phone, and it is pronounced just the way it looks.

Au revoir **Goodbye**. It's pronounced *oh rer-vwah*. Although if you say it quickly or don't pronounce it properly, you say *ov-wah*.

Oui, Non **Yes** and **No**. Pronounced *wee* and *noh*

Ouais This is funny. It's like saying **Yeah** instead of **Yes** (like your mother is always telling you to say it). It's pronounced *way*.

Monsieur Means **Mr**, as in 'Monsieur Greenwood likes to ride his bicycle,' and is pronounced *meh-sea-ur* but all joined together.

Madame Means **Mrs**, as in 'Madame Greenwood quickly prepared some courgette soup,' and is pronounced *mah-dahme*.

Mademoiselle	Means **Miss**, as in 'Mademoiselle Greenwood wanted to move to South America one day,' and is pronounced *mah-dem-mwa-zelle*.
Ça va? Ça va	It means both **How are you?** and **Yes I'm fine**. Pronounced *sah-vah?* And *sah-vah*.
Merci, Merci beaucoup	**Thank you, Thank you very much**. It is pronounced *merh-sea / merh-sea bohw-koo*.
Avec plaisir, De rien	When someone says thank you to you, you respond with **Avec plaisir – With pleasure** if you are from the south of France, or **De rien – It's nothing** if you are from the north of France (very generally of course). They are pronounced *a-veck play-zear*, and *der ree-ah*.
S'il vous plaît	Formal way to say **Please**. Translated word-for-word it means **If it you please** (or **If it pleases you**), and

	is pronounced *seel voo play*.
S'il te plaît	The informal way to say **Please** (to your friends, for example), and is pronounced *seel ter play*.
On y va, Vas y, Allez y	They all mean **Let's go.** Pronounced *oh nee vah, vah zee, a-lay zee*.
Quel dommage	**What a shame**, pronounced *kell doh-marhg*.
Ce n'est pas grave	**It's not important**, pronounced *snaye pah grahve*.
À tout a l'heure, À bientôt, À la prochaine	**See you very soon, See you soon, See you next time**. They are pronounced *ah toot a lehr / ah bee-en-toe / ah lah pro-chayne*.
Comment?	**What?** Literally translated it is **How?** but this is what the French people say when they are saying **What?** (pronounced *koh-mohn?*).
Donc, Alors	They both mean **So…**as in 'So, to continue…' They are pronounced *dohnk* and *ah-lorh*.
Youpi!	**Yahoo!** or **Yippee!** (pronounced *you-pee*). Those funny French!

Pas de souci	**No worries**. You hear this a lot. It is pronounced *pah'd soo-si*.
Tant pis	**Never mind**. A good response to some sad news of a minor nature. It is pronounced *tohn pee*.
Tant mieux	**That's great** (or literally, **So much the better**). Pronounced *tohn me-urh*.
C'est obligatoire	**You've got to do it**, and pronounced *set oh-bliig-a-twarh*. When my friend Thomas was little he didn't like to eat anything with chocolate in it; actually he preferred to eat spinach. One day his Mum gave him *mousse au chocolat* (chocolate mousse) for his dessert and he refused to eat it! (Can you believe it?!). His Mum said, 'Eat your *mousse au chocolat* Thomas! Now! *C'est obligatoire!*'
Mince!	**Oh bother!** It's pronounced *mahnce*.
M*e**	This means ***BEEP***. (Sorry I can't tell you – it's

a bad word.)

Zut alors! Means **Oh for goodness' sake!** And is pronounced *zoot ah-law*.

Aïe aïe aïe! Sort of means **Oh man!** It's pronounced *eye eye eye!*

Oh là là! It's an exclamation of surprise or shock or disbelief and is pronounced the way it looks. Sometimes when the French people say it it can go on a bit, **Oh là là là là là …!** Especially if it is a big surprise!

Chouette **Choice!** (pronounced *choo-et*). A lot of kids say it.

Doucement This means **Quietly** or **Softly**, and you hear the teachers saying it to the children at school – a lot! (pronounced *doo-ser-mohn*).

Vite! Vite! **Quick! Quick!** Mum is always saying that to us to get us to hurry up. It's pronounced *veet.*

Et voila! **And here it is!** As in 'Et voila! Here is the rabbit that had disappeared!' It is pronounced *eh vwa-lah.*

C'est tout   This means **That's all** (pronounced *say too*), and that's what I will end this little lesson with.

And don't forget - just say all of these words *wiz a veery 'eavy French akzent* (like Olivia) and you will be speaking French! AU REVOIR!

Appendix 7 Extra reading

Sixty Million Frenchmen Can't be Wrong by Jean-Benoît Nadeau & Julie Barlow

Allons Enfants by Linda Burgess

The Road from the Past by Ina Caro

My Life in France by Julia Child

The Little Prince (Le Petit Prince) by Antoine de St Exupéry

Fête Accomplie by Peta Mathias

French Toast by Peta Mathias

Salut! by Peta Mathias

A Year in Provence by Peter Mayle

Encore Provence by Peter Mayle

Toujours Provence by Peter Mayle

A Dog's Life by Peter Mayle

My Father's Glory by Marcel Pagnol

My Mother's Castle by Marcel Pagnol

The Time of Secrets by Marcel Pagnol

The Time of Love by Marcel Pagnol

Jean de Florette & Manon of the Springs by Marcel Pagnol

The Discovery of France by Graham Robb

The French Way by Ross Steele

A Certain Je Ne Sais Quoi by Charles Timoney

Pardon My French by Charles Timoney

Almost French by Sarah Turnbull

Afterword

In August 2009, at our goodbye-everyone party in Wellington, New Zealand, I loudly and boldly declared that I would not be writing blogs, or books, or newspaper articles or any such thing about our family's move to France, but rather I would send discreet little update emails, just occasionally; just when I had something really interesting to say.

But it didn't work out that way.

I found that the situations and challenges we were facing meant that I desperately needed some means by which to dump all my reflections and observations.

So I started writing ridiculously long and over-detailed emails to friends and family, with far too many photos attached.

And just to vary things, in one email I wrote a paragraph or two as if written by each of the children (then aged 9, 7 and 5 years old), in their own voice and style, chatting about their adventures, activities and associations, and what was important to them. I assumed their identities and wrote as they would speak.

I was surprised by the number of people who told me how much they enjoyed reading what the children had written and how they felt the children's personalities really shone through in the way *they* wrote.

Then one day, during a truly gorgeous birthday lunch at a two star Michelin restaurant by the name of 'Michel Sarran' in Toulouse with my lovely Richard, we engaged in a rather jolly, champagne-fuelled chat about our *progress to date* – leaving New Zealand, moving to France and finding our feet here, especially as we had not taken the 'expatriate, company pays all, accommodation taken care of, international schools for the children' route.

I thought then that there might be an amusing story in what we had experienced, but my question was this: how, *really*, is this different from all the other marvellous books about peoples' experiences in France?

I had read many, many books about France before we moved here, but only one book (*Allons Enfants* by Linda Burgess) dealt in any decent way about the experience of children moving to France. I really wanted to read more on that particular topic.

I pondered further as the weeks progressed but in the end I just started writing in order to capture my thoughts: three young children, a mature student husband, moving across the world, total immersion in a local French school, *very little to no language*, self-funding the adventure, finding our own accommodation, meeting the local French people, dealing with French officialdom, etc – all on a wing and a prayer.

One morning – to my surprise – I woke with my son Matthew's voice chattering away in my head. And his voice stayed with me.

And from that morning on I found myself observing and studying and critiquing and examining everything I saw, people I met, places I visited, buildings I noticed, languages I heard, with new eyes – from a 10-year-old boy's point of view – and significantly I found it was fun and refreshing, and a stimulating new perspective.

He went everywhere with me, and so I started recording *his* remarks as I wrote instead of my own rather ploddy deliberations.

Et voila! The true story called *Waking up in France* began; the story, as narrated by Matthew, of waking up to, and in, his new country with clear eyes and with striking and refreshing observations.

It has certainly been *no small thing* for us all to move to another country, where our native language is not widely or openly spoken and where we are the novelty-newcomers from the other side of the world.

But this book has been a wonderful means for me to be able to deal with our happenings and challenges, and to put it all to bed.

I was told by a friend that you needed to be in a new country a full year – for all four seasons – before you could possibly start to find your place in that new country.

For all of us, and especially for Matthew, I think it has taken more like two years – eight seasons.

And because of the complete lack of the local language thrown into the mix, the children have needed all of that time to assimilate the language in order to be able to get on with their lives and learning.

I cannot acknowledge and thank our children enough for so bravely tackling these new challenges and for joining in this adventure with vigour and pep, despite the undeniable difficulties.

Richard and I are very proud of them for the character they have shown in meeting these challenges.

And of course all thanks goes to my lovely Richard, for being my sounding-board and my encourager, and for being brave enough to start us on this extraordinary journey in the first place.

And, here we are now – happy, thriving, participating, absorbing, speaking, contributing, and becoming just a little bit more French.

All stories in this book are true.

Matthew has read the book and told me where some things were not quite right, and these have been corrected.

Some events he has forgotten, but I have used my knowledge of his young personality to express his thoughts and reactions to those different situations.

Some names of people throughout this book have been changed in order to protect privacy. Place names remain unchanged.

Sara Crompton Meade
15 December 2011
Ramonville St-Agne, France

Acknowledgements

Thank you of course to our wonderful children.

Thank you to my lovely Richard, for his sense of adventure and courage, and for his magnificent photographs throughout this book.

To the children's grandparents for their supportiveness about us moving to France, despite its immense distance from New Zealand and consequent lack of regular cuddles with their grandchildren.

To Mark and Maria Storey, Cathie and Stéphane Clatin, Anake Goodall (Matthew's godfather), and to all of our New Zealand friends for encouraging us to make the journey, and for great fun together.

To Alliance Française, Wellington, and to Dan and Anna Tait-Jamieson for their pearls of wisdom and their time.

To James for giving up his bed in the château for us, and to Paul and Sarah Hangartner for giving us wheels and so much useful advice for families living in France.

To Malin Arve for her thoroughly agreeable influence on us all, and for helping me on visits to various bureaucracies (and for the delicious lunches that followed such exhausting occasions).

To Samantha Vance for guiding me around Toulouse and for being an instant friend.

To Jerry Silverthorn for finding me the *normal* car.

To Marijo Huguet and Simone Raffin for all their help with French translations, and for ongoing and enjoyable French lessons, and friendship.

To Ramonville St-Agne for being a great place to live.

To the teachers and students of École Maternelle and École Élémentaire St Exupéry for their helpfulness and professionalism.

To Joanna Frew, Vivienne Holt, Sarah Rossiter-Pinfold, Erris Thompson and especially to Helen Crompton and Richard Meade for their interest, enthusiasm, suggestions and clever proofreading help with this manuscript. All remaining errors are my own.

To 'Annabelle', 'angel Patricia', 'Jeanne and Nicolas', and to 'Madame Durand' for working their various miracles.

To all of our wonderful French friends who have made us feel so welcome, especially the Huguet/Thomas family, the Laurell family, and the Swedish group in Toulouse - for letting Olivia and I pretend to be Swedish, and to Ross Jenkins for organising the wonderful fund-raising choirs at Puycelsi.

And to everyone who continues to graciously correct our French with nothing but kindness and encouragement (and the occasional giggle).

Author biography

Sara Crompton Meade was born and raised in New Zealand, and currently lives in Ramonville St-Agne, France, with her husband and three children. She has a degree in English and Psychology and various other diplomas that have occasionally been useful.

She has been writing inside her head for a long time to an imaginary but immensely appreciative audience, and this is her first book written for real people. She is determined that one day she will speak French quite well.

Read more about her and her family's adventures on: www.nzfrance.blogspot.com.

You can also contact her by emailing: nzfrance.stories@gmail.com.

www.saracromptonmeade.com